Valentina Harris, whose n[...] born in Rome and brough[...] by a large family of exc[...] stilled in her a real love [...] cooking. She holds the *Di[...] Cordon Bleu* from the Cordon Bleu Cookery School in Rome and she now lives in England with her two sons and her parents.

SOUTHERN ITALIAN COOKING

———— • ————

VALENTINA HARRIS

GRAFTON BOOKS

A Division of the Collins Publishing Group

————————————

LONDON GLASGOW
TORONTO SYDNEY AUCKLAND

Grafton Books
A Division of the Collins Publishing Group
8 Grafton Street, London W1X 3LA

A Grafton Paperback Original 1990

Copyright © Valentina Harris 1990

A CIP catalogue record for this book
is available from the British Library

ISBN 0-586-20855-0

Printed and bound in Great Britain by
Collins, Glasgow

Set in Futura

· CONTENTS ·

INTRODUCTION

Once beyond Rome, you could almost imagine yourself on another planet, let alone in another country. *Everything* changes in the south; different values and ideals take priority, and the endless sunlight makes it all appear bright, cheerful and colourful. Yet nothing is ever as it seems. The first of the five southern regions covered by this book is Campania, the area spread around Naples and the other major cities of the region. There is laughter and light on the surface here, yet just as the smooth, fertile soil conceals the mysteries of earthquakes and erupting volcanoes, so the smiling faces and joyful voices of Campania hide superstition, magic spells, frighteningly dark obsessions and fanatical religious beliefs. As you move further south these elements become stronger and more deeply entrenched. It is like a walk backwards in time, culminating with the extremely old-fashioned traditions of Sicily, where in the inland townships women are never seen walking alone outdoors unless they are on their way to church.

It is hard to describe accurately the atmosphere of southern Italy, and you cannot imagine what it is like even when you are sitting in an elegant café in a piazza in Turin. There is poverty, squalor, filth and disease in the south, together with housing problems and the constant threat of eruptions from the two volcanoes, Etna and Vesuvius. There is also age-old history, spun together with legends and folklore to create a fantastic, multi-faceted, wild and exciting tapestry which wraps itself about your soul from the second you alight in Naples and begin to explore and experience the south.

Never make the mistake of imagining the whole of the south to be as one. Each region has its own unique characteristics, which have developed as a result of the area's specific history. Apulia is like a slice of Greece. There is much to remind you of its past as part of the great Magna Graecia, and the almond blossom, olive groves and shepherds' whitewashed houses could be part of any Greek island. And yet this too is part of Italy; it is the most successful of the five regions and is developing commercially at great speed.

In Basilicata there is such an atmosphere of despair and misery that it seems to have seeped right into the barren soil. It will take nothing short of a miracle to wake up the region and bring it into the twenty-first century. But do you want it to be part of the twenty-first century? Perhaps it might be better to leave it to sleep quietly, preventing it where possible from falling into further disaster, but keeping it beautifully underdeveloped, rustic, savage and incredibly lovely. All too often, after years and years of neglect, corners of the south are developed almost overnight, with no thought for the local atmosphere. Then, just as suddenly as they appeared, the developers are gone and the eyesores are left behind.

Calabria is to me the most mysterious of all the southern regions. It even has its own brand of Mafia, about which even less is known than the Sicilian one. There is a cold, distant, austere quality about the people of Calabria, quite different from the usual image of southern Italians, and yet there is heat and passion here too.

A woman visiting anywhere in the south soon becomes accustomed to being eyed up like an object, even touched by complete strangers. She gets used to the narrowed eyes that slowly appraise her as she crosses the street or gets on a bus. She learns that what she wears or doesn't wear can cause her more trouble than it is worth. But nothing prepares her for Sicily, where the atmosphere becomes so arcane and mysterious that it's almost frightening. You can be certain that along with family honour, keeping the faith and their traditions, Sicilians are permanently tuned in to sex. Perhaps it's the sun which makes them so hot-blooded. Down here in the very deepest of the deep south it used to be common practice for a girl to have sex with her own father or eldest brother the night before she was wed, so that it would be certified that she was still a virgin and therefore the family honour was kept intact along with her purity. Who will ever know for certain if this pagan ritual is still performed, along with others that have been practised for centuries?

Just as the five regions have different characteristics and scenery, with a handful of common strands that tie them together, so the cuisine of the south varies greatly from area to area. The basic elements of southern cooking are the use of olive oil instead of butter, masses of fruit and vegetables, brilliant red tomatoes, and the general preference for fish rather than meat. Generally speaking the food of the south tends to have stronger flavours and be more colourful than the food of the north. Until very recently each one of the five regions was so separatist that to this very day, as you explore each one, you will discover differences and oddities that make it unique. Wherever you are in the south, you will discover things you never imagined were part of Italy. It is a world on its own that operates slowly under its own steam and by its own set of rules. Here the forces of history and the passage of time have moulded the land and created the people's unique outlook to such an extent that it will take another thousand years before anything really starts to change.

· CAMPANIA ·

It is in Campania that the very different face of southern Italy begins to form her expression. Not for Campania the steady somnolence of Apulia, the harsh and stunningly lovely arrogance of Calabria, the dry and empty beauty of Basilicata, or the sumptuous pomp of Sicily. This is the land of the wild tarantella, of la commedia dell'arte; the land where tomatoes became synonymous with Italian food after their introduction to the court of Naples in the sixteenth century; the land where no matter what happens, they'll soon be smiling again.

The centre of Campania is Naples, which is also its main city. You can form a very clear idea of the character of the entire region from this one city – and that is unusual in Italy. But in Naples' narrow, winding, squalid backstreets or along the boulevards around the busy, crowded port, beats the heart of the region. The *scugnizzo*, that scruffy, cheeky, wide-eyed street urchin, is to my mind the essence of this city. By the time they are eight, many children are working a ten- to twelve-hour day, often at something criminal. If I close my eyes and conjure up an image of Naples I always picture a small, thin boy in jeans and T-shirt, fag hanging out of the corner of his mouth, hands covered in dirty grease, enormous, brown, wise eyes laughing at me, and a tray of *caffé* balanced on the fingertips of one hand as he makes his way to his backstreet garage or electrical workshop. He is framed against a backdrop of brightly coloured washing flapping in the sunlight, strung between two tall, irregular, balconied blocks of flats, with bright plants flowering among the grime.

To fill your senses with the Campanian's typical sense of fun and expectation, walk the streets of any town or village in this region at midday and breathe in deeply the alluring scent of *ragù* bubbling gently over a flame – the brightest, sweetest, reddest *ragù* you are likely to find anywhere. Listen hard and you'll hear the sizzle of teasing, spattering batter that is frying crisp and golden round a filling that may be sweet, savoury, fishy or even cheesy – you never imagined food could look and smell so bright and cheerful, or tell you so much about the wonders of the people and the place that created it.

Stop and buy a piece of pizza from a roadside shop. The proper preparation of this ancient and noble dish is so close to Campanian hearts that there is a kind of classification in action, with special inspectors who visit restaurants to make sure the rules are being properly observed. A real pizza must be baked in a wood-burning oven constructed out of bricks and preferably set into the outside wall of a building, or freestanding like a barbecue. The further north you travel in Italy the thicker the base of the pizza will be. Here in Campania it is wafer thin and crisp, with a relatively thin layer of filling too.

Pizza is made all over the world and in many guises, all of which tend to turn it into something very far removed from the original version, the recipe for which appears on page 27. There is no Mozzarella and very little tomato, and there is certainly no sweetcorn, prawns, sausages, Stilton or curried mince such as might be found in some places! One of the most delicious and interesting pizzas created in this region is the very popular pizza Margherita. It was created in honour of Queen Margherita in the summer of 1889 when the royal couple were holidaying at Capodimonte (where the ceramics come from). The queen, who'd heard so much about pizza but had never eaten it, expressed her wish to try it. Don Raffaele Esposito, arguably the most brilliant of the world's pizza makers, came to the royal kitchen and prepared lots of different kinds of pizza for the king and queen, but the queen's favourite turned out to be the very simple Mozzarella, tomato and basil combination which so brilliantly symbolized the patriotism of its creator in his use of the colours of the national flag.

Pastry making is another great talent of the cooks of this region. Pastry chefs from these parts are in demand all over the world, so nimble and exacting are they in their technique. As in other parts of the south, the pastries and sweets of Campania are intricately shaped, delicious and addictive, be they baked or fried. I have not included very complicated recipes because I sincerely doubt whether any but the most dedicated cook would attempt to make them. However, if you are ever in Naples or its surroundings, make sure you stop off at a *pasticceria* and sample the delights of a *sfogliatella*, or *raffivoli*, intricate Neapolitan pastries with a rich filling.

When the humble tomato was first shown to the court on its arrival from South America it was viewed with immense suspicion and some fear. It was given the name *pomo d'oro*, meaning golden apple – in other words, it was thought to be the evil apple of the Garden of Eden. No cook in the country would touch it, but finally the impetuous, wild and crazy spirit of the Neapolitan took over – doubtless attracted by the tomato's brilliant colour and shiny, silky skin – and the whole flavour and feel of Italian cuisine was changed for ever. Nothing so perfectly encapsulates the core of Campanian cuisine as the bright red tomato, nowadays called *pomodoro* in the singular and *pomodori* or *pomidoro* in the plural. The perfectly formed San Marzano plum tomato, canned by the ton and exported to all corners of the earth by huge companies such as Cirio or Arrigoni, represents Campania's gold mine. This type of tomato doesn't grow anywhere other than in the province of Salerno, where 3,500 acres are dedicated to the cultivation of this marvellous plant. It doesn't lend itself to mechanized farming at all, so the old traditional methods of cultivation are used and the work has to be done mostly by hand. Each plant is held up by wiring to form neat rows with the fruits exposed to even sunlight and not resting against the soil. From June to September the tomato fever is at full pelt, the fields teeming with thousands of pickers filling basket after basket with San Marzano tomatoes. One-third of the annual production is sold fresh, while the rest is sold in bulk to canners. In order to keep the factories open all year round rather than just during the summer months, many of the local canning industries freeze some of the tomatoes until winter and then proceed to can them.

In Campania, the tomato is cooked lightly and quickly in order to retain all its brilliance, colour and freshness. It is perfect served with pasta, of course, but it is also used to enhance meat, fish, vegetables, seafood and Mozzarella cheese.

Golden mountains of crisp, deep-fried vegetables, fish, pizza, pastries, meat, or plain, delectable batter – this is another aspect of the cuisine of Campania. Its cooks have always been famous for their deep-frying, and their expertise is based on simple but rigorously observed rules. The end results are always crisp and full of flavour, never heavily greasy or overpowering.

For the Campanian cook, frying is a true art form and, despite all health considerations, one well worth learning. The rules are as follows:

1) The only type of oil that can be used more than once for frying is olive oil. All other types must be thrown away once used.

2) There must always be *plenty* of olive oil, other oil or fat. Enough to cover completely the food you are frying, and also enough to allow the food to float freely once it comes to the surface.

3) The oil or fat must be at its hottest point when the food is immersed in it, and should only subsequently be turned down to a lower heat.

4) All fried food must be carefully drained and all excess fat shaken off. It must also be kept warm until served.

Coffee is also very close to the heart and soul of the true Neapolitan – making coffee properly is something that has been written about, sung about, and generally viewed as an important social issue. Drinking that tiny cup of strong, pungent black coffee is as Neapolitan – and as Campanian – as the lush crop fields of Vesuvius. *La Napoletana* is a special local coffee percolator that allows the water to percolate up through the coffee, which is then turned over and the water drips slowly through a second time to make a very strong brew indeed. In this part of the world, coffee is drunk mainly first thing in the morning and after siesta time. It is savoured and enjoyed at the same slow pace with which it is prepared.

Cheese is another important feature of local cookery, and cheese in Campania really means the queen of all fresh cheeses, the delicious and extremely versatile Mozzarella. Other regions produce this cheese too, but it is here that they are the masters of making it, and it is of far better quality and flavour. The best is *Mozzarella di bufala*, which comes from water buffalo reared in the Piana del Dele. The locals go on family outings to Mondragone and Battipaglia specifically to buy these specially prepared fresh cheeses. The cow's-milk version is commonly known as *Fior di latte* and is more commonly used in cooking. How do you tell the difference? *Mozzarella di bufala* is bigger, fattier and has a bluish tint. Ordinary cow's-milk Mozzarella is chalk white and less fatty, and is made in several different shapes and sizes: *treccia* (plaited), *cigliege* (cherry-sized), etc. Also particularly good in this area are cheeses such as Caciocavallo and Pecorino. Both make excellent grating cheeses once matured and are used in many local recipes.

These then are the basic elements which make up the local cuisine – only a few, compared to areas further north, but everything is bursting with sunshine and good cheer, warmth, goodness and an intense vitality. *Ragù*, pizza, pastries, tomatoes, coffee, wonderful cheese, mountains of deep-fried delights of a hue that is as golden as sunlight – all washed down with wine as sparkling and mellow as the soft waves crashing along the shoreline, and all enhanced further by the marvellous vegetables and fruit, and the fresh riches of the sea.

Sunlight dances on the open markets, a sun that joins forces with the volcanic soil to give the region succulent fruit and vegetables that are bursting with flavour and goodness. There is certainly nothing mysterious about the local cuisine – it is all there for you to admire: at the markets, growing in the fields, hung between poles to dry in the hot sun, spread out on the quayside, arranged in the windows of the local shops, all with cheery artistry and bright and sunny colour schemes. However, the natural vivacity of the region has deep-seated and very strong undercurrents. Despite the clear-cut honesty of her table, Campania is a land of magic and mystery, of spells, witches and incantations, and of religious fanaticism. Behind the scenario of laughter and mandolins, ruby-red tomatoes, baskets of shimmering, silver fish and ripened fruit, are the terrible earthquakes and erupting volcanoes that have brought such devastating despair to the people of Campania for centuries.

The witches of the Benevento area are particularly well known. Their local brew, *liquore strega*, is named after them (some might say it tastes rather like a witch's potion) and the story behind the naming of the drink is fascinating.

The area is famous for many strange and mystical characters. Originally it was a Samnite settlement and bore the miserable name of Maleventum (bad event), but when the Romans overcame Pyrrhus and his elephants here in 275 B.C. it was decided to rename the town Beneventum in memory of the good event that had taken place. Thus Benevento came into being. Situated at the centre of a rich and fertile valley, and of immense strategic and commercial importance to the Romans, the town enjoyed many years of glory and splendour, particularly under the reign of Augustus. However, it was the Longobards who left it with a sinister and obscure legacy.

The Longobards used to gather outside the walls of the city under an old walnut tree and celebrate their pagan rites to the god Wotan. The Christians living inside the city exaggerated these occurrences out of all reasonable proportion, and soon rumours of everything from satanic masses to human sacrifices were attributed to the spot where the tree grew. Even long after the tree and the Longobards had gone, the stories and legends continued to proliferate. It became, supposedly, the place where all the local witches, wizards, demons and warlocks would gather to celebrate their meetings with the devil. Older people in this area still remember the superstitions connected to the walnut tree, and the other legends of these woods, such as the werewolf that prowls about when there is a full moon. For as long as anybody can remember, this province has had magical connotations. Until very recently there lived here many mystics, healers, and other 'magic people' to whom one could go for consultations, potions, spells or simply advice. These were real mystics who lived a life shrouded in mystery and suspense. Now that Italian witches and warlocks advertise regularly on television there seems to be less need for these old-timers and their dark powers, but it was the old-time witches who gave their name to the local liqueur.

The other provinces of Campania are Naples itself, Salerno, Caserta and Avellino. Within the province of Naples are the historical sites of Herculanum and Pompeii, as well as the holiday islands of Ischia and Capri. Caserta is famous for its gardens and fountains surrounding the Royal Palace of the Bourbons. Salerno contains the delightful town of Amalfi, which was once a marine republic of great power, and the Greek ruins of Paestum that date back over twenty-five centuries. Much of this area has been completely destroyed by the 1980 earthquake, which also affected a large part of the province of Avellino.

Despite all its hardships Campania has always and will always rise to live another day and tell another tale. No other place on earth has such an inbuilt capacity for survival, such a zest for life and such exuberance. The key word to the way of life in Campania is enjoyment, getting on with it no matter what the odds – and surely that is not so hard in a corner of the world surrounded by the sea and blessed with so many bountiful gifts from the land.

ANTIPASTI · ANTIPASTI

CROSTINI ALLA NAPOLETANA · NEAPOLITAN TOASTS

It is very unusual to discover butter in a cuisine that is so rich in fried dishes and that uses olive oil to enhance all its ingredients. When butter does crop up, as in this recipe, it is of exceptional quality and freshness and usually unsalted.

8 anchovy fillets, washed
125 g/4 oz unsalted butter, plus extra for greasing
8 thick slices white bread, crusts removed
2 small or 1 large Mozzarella cheese, thinly sliced into 16 pieces
4 ripe tomatoes, peeled, deseeded, and cut into 16 strips
salt and pepper
dried oregano

Cut each anchovy fillet in half so as to end up with 16 thin strips of fish. Soften the butter with a fork until it will spread easily. Cut the bread slices in half and spread each one thickly with butter on one side only, then top with a slice of Mozzarella, a strip of anchovy and a strip of tomato. Season with salt and pepper and a pinch of oregano and place on a buttered baking tray. Place in a preheated moderately hot oven (180°C, 350°F, Gas Mark 4) for 8–10 minutes then serve at once as a delicious antipasto.

Serves 4

MOZZARELLA IN CARROZZA · MOZZARELLA IN A CARRIAGE

Mozzarella in a carriage, the dish that is almost as Neapolitan as pizza itself. The housewives and cooks of these parts have for centuries been famous for their ability to fry lightly and evenly. That is the secret of this delicious dish, which should never taste as if it has been soaked in gallons of oil. Serve as a starter or main course, or make them much smaller and serve with drinks.

> **8 thick slices white bread, crusts removed**
> **1 large Mozzarella cheese, thickly sliced**
> **300 ml/½ pint cold water**
> **2 level tablespoons plain white flour**
> **2 eggs, thoroughly beaten**
> **salt**
> **olive oil for frying (about 7.5 cm/3 inches deep in a**
> **25 cm/10 inch frying pan)**

Take 4 slices of the bread and cover them thickly with Mozzarella slices, making sure the cheese does not go over the edges. Cover each one with the remaining slices of bread and press down hard with your hand to close each sandwich. Put the cold water in a wide bowl and the flour on a flat plate. Carefully dip each side of each sandwich in the cold water, then in the flour – this forms a kind of glue that stops the Mozzarella escaping when you fry the sandwiches, but it must not become stodgy and overpowering. Lay each sealed sandwich in a deep platter and pour over the beaten eggs, seasoned with a little salt. Leave to soak for 10 minutes then very carefully turn the sandwiches over and leave for a further 10 minutes. Heat the oil until sizzling, then fry the four 'carriages' until golden and crisp, turning over halfway through. Drain on paper before serving hot.

Serves 4

TARALLI COL PEPE · CALABRIAN BISCUITS

Spicy, savoury biscuits to nibble on while you await the rest of your meal are very popular in Campania. A delicious alternative is to make these with caraway seeds instead of pepper, and they also tend to be more digestible that way.

> **625 g/1 lb 4 oz fine white flour**
> **30 g/1¼ oz fresh yeast, diluted in a little tepid water to a smooth, wet paste**
> **salt**
> **freshly ground black pepper**
> **200 g/7 oz lard**
> **50 g/2 oz almonds, blanched, peeled and cut in half**

Put 125 g/4 oz of the flour in a bowl and add the yeast mixture. Knead together to form a smooth, round ball, place in a floured bowl, cover with a napkin and leave in a warm place to rise for 1 hour until doubled in size. Then put the risen dough back on the worktop, add the remaining 500 g/1 lb flour, a pinch of salt, plenty of freshly ground black pepper to taste and 175 g/6 oz of the lard. Knead together carefully, adding just enough water to make the dough the same consistency as bread dough. Roll it up into a ball again and put into a large bowl. Cover with a napkin and leave in a warm place to rise for about 1 hour. When the dough has doubled in size, turn out on to the worktop again and roll out thinly, then cut into sticks about 16 cm/6 inches long. Take three at a time and plait them together, then coil each plait neatly into a circle. Grease a baking tray with the remaining lard. Lay the plaited circles on the baking tray and decorate them with the almonds, pushing each half nut deep into the dough with only its top sticking out. Cover with a napkin and leave to rise once more until they have doubled in volume. Bake in a pre-heated very low oven (100°C, 200°F, Gas Mark ¼) for one hour, making sure they do not colour.

Makes about 26

LE MINESTRE · SOUP

ZUPPA DI ZUCCHINE · COURGETTE SOUP

In Italy the humble courgette changes sex depending upon where it comes from! In the south it is quite definitely female – *zucchina*, plural *zucchine* – whereas further up the leg of the boot it appears as a single *zucchino* and a whole team of *zucchini*. In any case, this is a soup to be served during the heat of the summer, when there are plenty of sweet courgettes around and hot soups are not at all what is wanted to eat. It makes the most of the delightfully fresh flavour and tender texture of courgettes, creating a soup that is nourishing and wholesome without being too filling or heavy on the digestion.

> **50 g/2 oz lard**
> **4 tablespoons olive oil**
> **5 medium-sized courgettes, washed and diced**
> **1.2 litres/2 pints water**
> **salt and pepper**
> **½ a French loaf, cut into 2.5 cm/1 inch slices**
> **2 eggs**
> **25 g/1 oz fresh parsley, chopped**
> **25 g/1 oz fresh basil, torn into shreds**
> **3 tablespoons grated Parmesan cheese**

In a fairly big saucepan, heat the lard and the olive oil together until just sizzling, then add the diced courgettes. Turn and fry for a few minutes, then add the water. Season with salt and pepper, place a lid on the saucepan and leave to boil gently for 45 minutes. Meanwhile prepare the bread by gently toasting each slice under the grill or in the oven until crisp and biscuity in texture. When the courgettes are soft, break the eggs into a bowl and add the herbs and Parmesan. Beat together thoroughly, then pour into the soup. Stir carefully until the eggs are just cooked, then remove the saucepan from the heat. Place the toasted bread in the bottom of a soup tureen and pour the soup over it. Leave to cool until just tepid, then serve.

Serves 4

PASTA · PASTA

TIMBALLO DI MACCHERONI · BAKED MACARONI TIMBALE

The people of these parts have been famous for many centuries for being great *maccheroni* eaters. The word *maccheroni* is to some extent a collective name for pasta in Campania, whereas in other regions of Italy it refers exclusively to short, stubby, hollow, tube-shaped pasta. Unlike timbales made elsewhere in Italy this one does not have a pastry casing around the outside. It is a real 'special-occasion' dish with lots of fabulous flavours and textures.

> 25 g/1 oz porcini (dried mushrooms)
> 125 g/4 oz butter
> 7 tablespoons fresh breadcrumbs
> 1 egg, beaten
> 250 g/8 oz chicken giblets, cleaned and coarsely chopped
> 400 g/13 oz canned tomatoes, drained, deseeded and chopped
> pinch of cinnamon
> pinch of allspice
> pinch of nutmeg
> salt and pepper

400 g/13 oz rigatoni (lined macaroni)
1 medium-sized, fresh or canned black truffle, thinly sliced

Cover the mushrooms with tepid water and leave them to soak. Use some of the butter to grease a 6-serving timbale mould thoroughly, then dust thickly with some of the breadcrumbs. Pour the beaten egg over the breadcrumbs and swill it around to cover and stick on the breadcrumb surface. Then cover the egg layer with more breadcrumbs.

Place the chicken giblets in a pan with the remaining butter. Fry them together gently. Drain and dry the mushrooms and add them to the saucepan. Fry for 2–3 minutes over a low heat, then add the tomatoes. Season with the spices, salt and pepper, and leave to simmer slowly until required. Bring a large pot of salted water to the boil. Meanwhile remove just the giblets from the sauce. Set these aside. Put the pasta into the boiling water and cook until half done (about 5 minutes – see instructions on the packet as cooking times vary according to the brand), remove from the heat and drain thoroughly, then return to the pot in which it was cooked. Dress the pasta with the tomato sauce, then pour half the pasta into the timbale mould. Spoon the giblets and the sliced truffle on top then cover with the rest of the pasta. Cover the top of the mould with an oiled sheet of greaseproof paper and bake in a preheated warm oven (160°C, 325°F, Gas Mark 3) for 1 hour. Then remove the timbale from the oven and leave to cool for 5 minutes. Run a knife quickly around the edges of the mould and turn the timbale out on to a platter to serve.

Serves 6

PIZZA · PIZZA

PIZZELLE FRITTE ALLA NAPOLETANA · LITTLE NEAPOLITAN FRIED PIZZAS

As with many dishes from the south, the deceptively simple appearance of these little pizzas belies the amount of work and care that has gone into creating them. In this case the two greatest traditions of the region's cuisine – pizza making and frying – are brought together in one single recipe, and the result is absolutely delightful.

> **200 g/7 oz plain white flour**
> **175 ml/7 fl oz water**
> **salt and pepper**
> **1 egg, separated**
> **200 g/7 oz lean prosciutto crudo (Parma ham), thickly sliced, *or* 125 g/4 oz anchovy fillets**
> **oil for deep frying**

Put the flour into a bowl and add the water and seasoning. Beat together energetically with a fork for at least 5 minutes, then add the egg yolk and beat for a further 5 minutes. Whisk the egg white until stiff and fold it into the mixture. Cut the prosciutto slices, if using, into thick strips, about the size of a finger. Heat the oil for frying. Immerse each piece of prosciutto or each anchovy fillet in the dough then scoop out with a large spoon, taking as much of the dough with the prosciutto or anchovy as you can. Fry the *pizzelle* in the oil until crisp and crunchy. Serve hot as an informal starter with a light sprinkling of salt and a tomato salad.

Serves 4

LA PIZZA · PIZZA

This is the original, genuine pizza Napoletana. All other kinds of pizza are merely variations on this basic theme. Note that there is no Mozzarella, no anchovies and very little tomato.

> **200 g/7 oz bread dough, fully risen (see basic recipe, page 218)**
> **6 canned tomatoes, drained and cut into strips**
> **pinch of dried oregano**
> **5 fresh basil leaves, cut into strips or torn**
> **1 clove garlic, chopped**
> **6 tablespoons olive oil (more if desired)**
> **salt**

Lay the bread dough on the worktop and flatten it out with your hands to give a round shape slightly larger than a dinner plate. Place on an oiled baking tray and dress with the tomato strips, oregano, basil and garlic, covering the whole surface but leaving a border – *il cornicione* – of about 2.5 cm/1 inch all the way round. Pour the oil over the pizza, drenching it really thoroughly. Season with a little salt and place in the centre of a preheated hot oven (200°C, 400°F, Gas Mark 6) for about 8 minutes or until the border is crisp and browned. Serve immediately.

Serves 1

IL CALZONE · PAIR OF TROUSERS

The inimitable 'pair of trousers' remains one of my real favourites if it is cooked correctly. Essentially it is a pizza with its filling on the inside, the dough being folded over like an envelope. Like all pizzas, it is important that the balance of ingredients should be absolutely right. *Calzone* can be made either as one large item or several small ones, and can also be deep fried. I personally find it easier to fry rather than bake this dish at home, where the classic brick, wood-fired, outdoor bread oven vital to pizza making simply isn't available, although many Italian households build one specially for this purpose.

> **625 g/1 lb 4 oz bread dough, fully risen (see basic recipe, page 218)**
> **125 g/4 oz fresh Ricotta cheese, sieved**
> **1 egg**
> **salt**
> **5 tablespoons grated Parmesan cheese**
> **125 g/4 oz salame, diced**
> **125 g/4 oz Mozzarella cheese, diced**
> **oil for greasing**

Flatten the dough out with your hands until it is about 0.5 cm/ ¼ inch thick. Mix together the Ricotta, egg, salt, Parmesan, salame and Mozzarella. Spoon it over half the flattened dough, towards the centre. Fold the dough in half and pinch round the edges to keep all the filling inside. Grease a baking tray and carefully lay the *calzone* on it. Place in the centre of a preheated hot oven (200°C, 400°F, Gas Mark 6) and bake for about 30 minutes. Serve very hot.

Serves 4

PIZZA ALLA CAMPOFRANCO · CAMPOFRANCO PIZZA

This is a deliciously fragrant, rich and golden pizza with its delectable filling secure on the inside. I find it is one member of the pizza family that really does work in a domestic gas or electric oven.

325 g/11 oz plain white flour
1½ level tablespoons sugar
salt
175 g/6 oz butter, softened and diced
5 egg yolks
4 egg whites
20 g/¾ oz yeast, diluted in a little warm milk
2 tablespoons olive oil
5 large ripe tomatoes, peeled, deseeded and quartered
pepper
lard for greasing
5 fresh basil leaves, chopped or torn
2 small Mozzarella cheeses, chopped
175 g/6 oz prosciutto crudo (Parma ham), chopped
6 tablespoons grated Parmesan cheese
2 tablespoons grated Pecorino cheese

Place 300 g/10 oz of the flour on a worktop, keeping the rest to one side to help you work. Mix the sugar and salt in with your hands, then draw the flour together into a mountain and make a hole in the middle with your fist. Put the butter, 4 of the egg yolks, the 4 egg whites and the diluted yeast into the hole and work the dough together very thoroughly until you have a really smooth and elastic consistency. Place in a floured bowl, cover with a napkin and put somewhere warm to rise for about 3 hours or until doubled in bulk.

Heat the olive oil in a pan and add the tomatoes. Season with salt and pepper and cook until soft without breaking them up. Put the dough back on to a floured worktop and divide in two, one piece slightly larger than the other. Knead gently for a few minutes, then roll each one out. Grease a 25 cm/10 inch shallow cake tin with lard and line it with the larger piece of dough. Fill with the tomatoes, basil, Mozzarella, prosciutto and finally the grated cheeses. Cover with the other piece of dough and seal the edges carefully by folding the dough under and pinching it together all the way round. Beat the remaining egg yolk and brush the top of the pizza with it. Bake in a preheated hot oven (200°C, 400°F, Gas Mark 6) for 30–40 minutes. Serve very hot.

Serves 6

IL RISO · RICE

SARTÙ DI RISO · BAKED RICE TIMBALE

On the rare occasions when rice is eaten in the south, it is in the form of remarkable sculpted creations such as this one, with varying degrees of complication. This recipe appears here in the original version, although nowadays the modern housewife or cook will prepare the same in a much less complicated and rich dish; however, the style of presentation is always identical.

> 25 g/1 oz porcini (dried mushrooms)
> 1 small onion, finely chopped
> 4 tablespoons olive oil
> 2 tablespoons tomato paste, diluted in 1 wine glass hot broth
> 250 g/8 oz fresh peas (shelled weight)
> salt and pepper
> 6 pork sausages
> 300 g/10 oz minced beef
> 3 eggs
> 8 heaped tablespoons grated Parmesan cheese
> 3 heaped tablespoons fresh breadcrumbs
> oil for deep frying
> 3 level tablespoons plain white flour
> 400 g/13 oz risotto rice
> 1.5 litres/2½ pints broth, kept boiling hot

200 g/7 oz lard
200 g/7 oz chicken livers, cleaned and coarsely
chopped
1 large Mozzarella cheese, diced

Cover the mushrooms in warm water and set them aside to soak until soft. Fry the onion in the oil, preferably in a terracotta pot, until translucent, then add the diluted tomato paste. Stir together, and simmer for 4 minutes.

Meanwhile strain the mushrooms and chop finely. Add the peas, mushrooms, salt and pepper to the simmering sauce; stir and taste for seasoning. Then lay the sausages in the sauce and cook for about 20 minutes. Remove the sausages, slice thinly, and set aside. Put the minced beef in a bowl, add seasoning, 1 egg, 1 tablespoon grated Parmesan and 1 tablespoon bread-crumbs. Mix together carefully, then shape into balls the size of walnuts. Heat the oil for deep frying. Toss the meatballs in the flour and fry in the hot oil until brown, then drain on kitchen paper and keep to one side.

Pour just over half the prepared tomato and pea sauce into a deep saucepan over a medium heat. As soon as it gets really hot add the rice and turn it over in the sauce. Start adding the hot broth a little at a time until the rice is cooked (about 20 minutes), stirring frequently. When the rice is tender, mix in the two remaining eggs, 4 tablespoons of grated Parmesan and 50 g/ 2 oz of the lard. Stir thoroughly to distribute all these ingredients evenly, then set the risotto aside to cool down. Place over a medium flame a small pan containing 20 g/¾ oz of the lard. When the lard is sizzling, add the chicken livers and cook quickly to brown them all over, then remove from the heat and season.

Grease a 3 litre/5 pint timbale mould with half the remaining lard and scatter half the remaining breadcrumbs over it. Pour almost all the risotto into the mould and push it out towards the edges and sides to make it hollow in the centre. In the central hollow, start layering the various ingredients as follows: first some of the meatballs, then a little of the sauce, a few chicken livers, slices of cooked sausages and the Mozzarella. Cover with grated Parmesan and begin again with the meatballs until you have used everything up. Cover finally with all the remaining risotto. Smooth the surface carefully with a knife, scatter a few pieces of lard and the remaining breadcrumbs over the surface and place in a preheated warm oven (160°C, 325°F, Gas Mark 3) for about 30 minutes. Remove from the oven and leave to cool for a few minutes, then turn out on to a platter and serve at once.

Serves 6

I LEGUMI · VEGETABLES

CIANFOTTA · CAMPANIAN VEGETABLE STEW

One of my favourite southern dishes is this wonderfully sweet vegetable stew. It is marvellously bright and colourful, bursting with flavour and sunshine.

    2 medium-sized aubergines
    salt
    300 g/10 oz canned tomatoes or very ripe fresh
    tomatoes, peeled
    750 g/1 lb 8 oz potatoes, peeled
    500 g/1 lb onions, peeled
    2 large courgettes
    6 fresh basil leaves
    1 celery stick
    ½ wine glass olive oil
    750 g/1 lb 8 oz yellow peppers

Cut the aubergines into squares, put them in a colander, sprinkle with salt and put the colander into the sink so that the bitter juices will drain out. Leave for at least 1 hour. Sieve the tomatoes. Cut the potatoes into squares the same size as the aubergines. Slice the onions fairly thickly, top and tail and slice the courgettes. Chop the basil and the celery together. Heat the oil in a terracotta or metal saucepan and add the celery and basil. Fry gently together, then add the onions and fry until soft. Add the tomatoes, and as soon as the mixture begins to simmer add the potatoes. Rinse the aubergines, pat them dry and add them to the pan. Add the courgettes and season to taste. Cover and simmer on the lowest possible heat. Stir often, adding a little water if the stew appears to be drying out too much. Cut the peppers in half, remove the seeds and cut them into thin strips. When the potatoes are almost cooked add the peppers and cook until tender. Leave to cool completely and serve with just a little olive oil sprinkled over the top.

Serves 4

PARMIGIANA DI MELANZANE · BAKED AUBERGINES WITH MOZZARELLA AND TOMATOES

Although many of the southern regions claim to have invented this dish, there is no doubt that it is really a Campanian speciality. In some areas of the region a thin layer of melted bitter chocolate is included. This strange combination of bitter chocolate with sweet aubergine crops up quite often in southern cooking. Perhaps the reason is that the aubergine arrived from the Arab world and continued to be cooked with traditional Arab extravagance and imagination even in the sixteenth century when the cocoa bean finally arrived from South America.

**4 large aubergines
1 onion, finely chopped**

> 3 tablespoons olive oil
> 4 fresh basil leaves, chopped or torn
> 600 ml/1 pint passata (puréed tomatoes)
> salt and pepper
> 5 tablespoons flour
> oil for deep frying
> 9 tablespoons grated Parmesan cheese
> 2 eggs, hardboiled and sliced
> 1 large Mozzarella cheese, sliced

Slice the aubergines to about 1 cm/½ inch thickness, then lay them in a colander and sprinkle with salt. Put the colander in the sink and let the bitter juices drain out. Leave for at least 1 hour, then rinse and pat dry. Meanwhile fry the onion in the olive oil until translucent. Add the basil and passata, season and cook gently for 30 minutes. Remove from the heat. Toss the aubergine slices briefly in the flour and deep fry until golden, then drain on kitchen paper. Line a greased ovenproof dish with some of the fried aubergines and scatter a little of the grated Parmesan over them. Then add a layer of sliced egg, a layer of sliced Mozzarella and a layer of tomato sauce. Begin again with a layer of aubergines, then Parmesan, egg, Mozzarella, sauce and so on until you have used all the ingredients up. The last layer must be tomato sauce. Place in a preheated moderate oven (180°C, 350°F, Gas Mark 4) for about 30 minutes. Allow to cool before serving, although it can also be served hot.

Serves 4

ZUCCHINE ALLA BELLA NAPOLI · COURGETTES IN THE STYLE OF BEAUTIFUL NAPLES

This is very similar to the *parmigiana* made with aubergines, as they both contain tomato and melted Mozzarella. There the likeness ends because this dish has a wonderful freshness and lightness about it that the more hearty and substantial aubergine dish doesn't possess.

     6 large courgettes
     50 g/2 oz lard
     3 tablespoons olive oil
     1 very small onion, thinly sliced
     500 g/1 lb canned tomatoes, drained, deseeded and
     chopped, or equivalent fresh tomatoes, peeled
     salt and pepper
     1 sprig fresh oregano
     4 tablespoons flour
     oil for deep frying
     2 medium-sized Mozzarella cheeses, thinly sliced

Slice the courgettes thickly and lay them in rows on a platter. Salt them, then put the platter on a slant over the sink for about 1 hour so all the courgettes' juices drain out. Meanwhile fry the lard, olive oil and onion together until the onion is translucent. Add the tomatoes, salt, pepper and oregano. Stir, then cover and simmer gently for 1 hour. Remove from the heat and sieve. Rinse and dry the courgettes and toss in the flour, then deep fry until golden. Drain on kitchen paper. Line a greased ovenproof dish with fried courgettes and cover with slices of Mozzarella, then with tomato sauce. Add another layer of courgettes and so on until you end up with a final layer of Mozzarella and tomato sauce. How many layers depends upon the shape of your dish. Place in a pre-heated moderate oven (180°C, 350°F, Gas Mark 4) for 20 minutes. Serve piping hot.

Serves 4

FAGIOLI ALLA MARUZZARA · MARUZZARA BEANS

For this dish to be authentic, the bread should be sliced from a
palata or *San Giovannese* loaf. These enormous loaves weigh
up to 2 kg/4 lb each and occupy the entire length of the *pala*, the
long-handled spade used to slide bread or pizza into the glow-
ing centre of the oven. San Giovanni used to be patron saint of
the area of countryside around Naples, so this is really the
closest thing to a country loaf in local terms.

> **1.2 kg/2 lb 7 oz fresh or dried cannellini beans (canned
> beans are not suitable)**
> **1 celery stick, cut into thin strips**
> **salt and pepper**
> **500 g/1 lb fresh ripe tomatoes, peeled, deseeded and
> coarsely chopped**
> **125 g/4 oz olive oil**
> **fistful of fresh parsley, chopped**
> **2 cloves garlic, chopped**
> **pinch of dried oregano**
> **8 slices coarse white bread**

If using dried beans, soak them overnight and boil very quickly
for 5 minutes. Then drain and rinse them and continue as
described below.

Place the beans in a pot, cover with cold water and bring to the
boil. Simmer very slowly for about 30 minutes, then add the
celery. Continue to simmer very slowly for about 45 minutes or
until the beans are really soft. Then add the seasoning, tomatoes,
olive oil, parsley, garlic and oregano. Stir through and remove
from the heat. Put the slices of bread in the bottom of a serving
dish and pour the beans over the bread. Leave for 5 minutes then
serve.

Serves 4

I PESCI · FISH

POLPO ALLA LUCIANA · OCTOPUS LUCIANA'S STYLE

This method of cooking octopus was apparently invented by the fishermen of the Santa Lucia district. Ideally you should use a *verace* octopus, in other words one with a double row of suckers on its tentacles. If several baby octopus are used instead of one big one, the resulting dish is called *purpelle affocate* (drowned baby octopus).

> 1 kg/2 lb fresh octopus
> salt and pepper
> 4 canned tomatoes, drained, deseeded and chopped
> 1 wine glass olive oil
> 3 cloves garlic, finely chopped
> fistful of fresh parsley, finely chopped

If the octopus is not neatly cleaned and prepared I am afraid that you will have to carry out this operation yourself. Holding it very firmly in your hand, slap it repeatedly on a hard surface – preferably stone or marble – for approximately 30 minutes to tenderize it. Alternatively, rub it hard on the inside of a basket for about 15 minutes. Then remove its eyes, mouth and bladder and wash extremely carefully in running water. You may, of course, need more than 1 octopus to make up the weight. Place the octopus in a terracotta saucepan, season generously with salt and pepper and scatter the tomatoes over it. Pour in the glass of olive oil and cover the top of the saucepan tightly with tinfoil. Tie a piece of string around the tinfoil on the outside of the saucepan and put the lid on top. Cook over a medium heat for 2 hours, then remove the lid and the tinfoil and scatter the garlic and parsley over the finished dish. To be authentic you must serve the octopus from the pot in which it was cooked, and you can serve it hot or cold.

Serves 4

SARDE ALLA NAPOLETANA · NEAPOLITAN SARDINES

A delicious and very simple dish of sardines, which retains all the brilliant red of the local tomatoes, the freshness of the fish and the tang of the herbs and garlic. It is a wonderful dish whether served hot or cold.

> **625 g/1 lb 4 oz fresh sardines, gutted**
> **8 tablespoons olive oil**
> **salt and pepper**
> **large pinch of dried oregano**
> **3 large ripe tomatoes, peeled, deseeded and cut into strips**
> **2 cloves garlic, finely chopped**
> **4 tablespoons chopped fresh parsley**

Remove the heads from the sardines, wash and clean them with great care, then dry them on a kitchen towel and set aside. Pour 6 tablespoons of the olive oil into a shallow ovenproof dish and lay the fish in it, keeping them close together. Season generously with salt, pepper and oregano, put the strips of tomato round the edges of the fish to frame them, then scatter the garlic and parsley over. Dribble the remaining olive oil over the fish and tomatoes then place in a preheated hot oven (200°C, 400°F, Gas Mark 6). Bake for 20 minutes and serve either hot or cold. Sardines prepared in this way are really delicious.

Serves 4

VONGOLE ALLA NAPOLETANA · NEAPOLITAN CLAMS

Fish and seafood simply cooked, often with tomatoes for colour and added sweetness, form the basis of many a memorable meal in Campania, and this is no exception to the rule. The delicious little *vongole* (baby clams) are cooked just long enough to make them open up (any that do not open up MUST be thrown away as they are not safe to eat) and, with the addition of tomatoes, olive oil, parsley and garlic, make a dish that is a cross between a soup and a stew. It is eaten mostly with the fingers – a sensual, lingering meal to be enjoyed and never hurried.

> **1 kg/2 lb live clams**
> **3 cloves garlic**
> **fistful of fresh parsley**
> **125 g/4 oz olive oil**
> **400 g/13 oz canned tomatoes, drained and chopped**
> **salt**
> **freshly ground black pepper**

Scrub the clams carefully one by one if they appear particularly muddy or sandy. Then put them in a basin of cold salted water for 1 hour, stirring occasionally – this will make them open up and exude any sand or grit that may be trapped inside the shell. Meanwhile chop the garlic and the parsley and fry gently in the olive oil until soft. Then add the tomatoes and cook for 10 minutes. Add salt and remove from the heat. Drain the clams, wash carefully and drain again. Add the clean clams to the tomato mixture and heat through quickly. As soon as all the clams have opened up, add a generous grinding of black pepper and serve. They should take a maximum of six minutes to open up – any shells that are still closed after this time will not open at all and must be thrown away.

Serves 4

MPEPATA DI COZZE · PEPPERED MUSSELS

A fiery dish of deliciously fresh mussels with a coating of freshly ground black pepper – the essence of southern Italian cuisine is that the raw materials are so fresh and succulent you need little else to finish the dish.

40–50 fresh mussels
juice of 1 lemon
freshly ground black pepper
fistful of parsley, finely chopped

Scrub, wash and de-beard the mussels carefully, then place in a saucepan with a ladleful of water. Put the saucepan over a medium heat and shake so that all the mussels gradually heat and open up. Remove the mussels from the pan, tear off the empty top shells and discard, then set the mussels aside. Strain the liquid from the pan into a bowl through a fairly thick muslin cloth and leave to settle. Wash the pan and pour the strained liquid back into it, being careful not to let the sediment into the pan. Arrange all the mussels in their half shells back in the pan and pour the lemon juice over them. Grind plenty of black pepper over the mussels, then scatter the parsley over. Warm through over a lively heat for a few minutes, then serve.

Serves 4

LE CARNI · MEAT

POLPETTONE ALLA NAPOLETANA · NEAPOLITAN MEATLOAF

A wonderfully rich and succulent meat dish in a part of the country where meat is really used very little. All the expertise and flair of the Neapolitan cook is here in this marvellous meat loaf.

150 g/5 oz fresh white bread, crusts removed
1 heaped tablespoon sultanas
1 large slice beef (preferably rump), weighing
500 g/1 lb
salt and pepper
140 g/4½ oz prosciutto crudo (Parma ham), chopped
fistful of fresh parsley, chopped
2 cloves garlic, chopped
2 egg yolks
1 heaped tablespoon pine nuts
50 g/2 oz lard
1 clove
1 onion, chopped
1 carrot, chopped
1 celery stick, chopped
1 tablespoon tomato paste, diluted in a little hot water

Soak the bread in a little water then squeeze it between your hands and set to one side in a bowl. Cover the sultanas with cold water and leave to soak for not more than 15 minutes. Meanwhile flatten the beef out as much as possible with a meat hammer or the flat side of a heavy knife. Season with salt and pepper. Weigh out 100 g/3½ oz of the prosciutto crudo and scatter it over the beef. Mix the bread with the parsley, garlic and egg yolks and spread over the beef and prosciutto. Strain the sultanas and scatter them over the mixture, then sprinkle the pine nuts over that. Roll the beef up and tie the ends securely with butcher's string. Put the lard and the remaining prosciutto into an oval casserole and fry for about 5 minutes over a gentle heat, then lay the beef roll on the top. Raise the heat and brown the meat on all sides, then add the clove, onion, carrot and celery. Lower the heat, cover and simmer for about 15 minutes or until all the vegetables have become completely soft. Then add the diluted tomato paste. Cover and simmer on the lowest possible heat for about 2 hours, then remove the meat and leave to rest for 5 minutes. Cut off the string, cut the meat into thick slices and arrange on a warmed serving platter. Sieve or blend the sauce remaining in the casserole and pour it over the meat. Serve with mashed potatoes to soak it all up. Or reserve some of the sauce and use for dressing some pasta if you wish.

Serves 4

COSTATA ALLA PIZZAIOLA · BEEF WITH PIZZAIOLA SAUCE

A very original way of preparing a plain beef steak. The ingredients found in so many Campanian dishes – tomatoes, garlic, oil and oregano – are used here to bring a slice of meat to life.

> **2 slices of beef cut from the forerib without the bone, weighing approximately 1 kg/2 lb altogether**
> **7 tablespoons olive oil**
> **700 g/1 lb 7 oz canned tomatoes, drained, deseeded and chopped, or equivalent fresh tomatoes, peeled and deseeded**
> **4 cloves garlic, finely chopped**
> **½ heaped teaspoon dried oregano**
> **salt and pepper**

Flatten the beef as much as possible. Heat the oil in a wide pan until sizzling. Fry the meat quickly in the oil, browning it on both sides. Then scatter the tomatoes and garlic over the meat. Sprinkle over the oregano, salt and pepper, then cover. Simmer very slowly for about 15 minutes until the tomatoes are reduced to a smooth, thick sauce. Lay the meat on a platter, cover with the sauce and serve.

Serves 4

BRACIOLE DI MAIALE ALLA NAPOLETANA · PORK OLIVES, NEAPOLITAN STYLE

    8 slices pork loin, weighing approximately 900 g/
    1 lb 13 oz altogether
    50 g/2 oz seedless raisins
    125 g/4 oz prosciutto crudo (Parma ham)
    50 g/2 oz capers, chopped
    50 g/2 oz pine nuts, chopped
    1 tablespoon fresh breadcrumbs
    4 tablespoons olive oil
    50 g/2 oz lard
    ½ chilli pepper
    1 tablespoon tomato paste, diluted in a little warm
    water
    salt and pepper

Flatten the pieces of pork until as thin as possible, then trim the edges to square them up. Soak the raisins in a little water for 15 minutes, then drain and dry thoroughly. Chop the pork trimmings with the prosciutto very finely, then add the capers, pine nuts, raisins and breadcrumbs. Mix together very carefully, then spread the mixture over each slice of pork. Roll up and secure with a wooden toothpick.

Heat the oil and lard together in a pan until sizzling, then fry the meat in the pan until browned on all sides. Add the ½ chilli pepper and the diluted tomato paste, cover and simmer gently for about 2 hours, stirring frequently and adding warm water if it appears to be drying out too much. Season. Remove the pork olives from the saucepan, take out the toothpicks and arrange the meat on a platter. Pour over the sauce and serve at once.

Serves 6

AGNELLO PASQUALE · EASTER LAMB

Easter is celebrated with a lamb dish in almost all parts of Italy. In this case the dish is deliciously simple and easy to cook. There is one common point in all these recipes and that is that the cooking of all these dishes takes place over a very low flame or in a cool oven – the cooking time is always slow to enable all the flavours to mingle and develop.

> **Shoulders or legs of a very young spring lamb, weighing altogether approximately 1.2 kg/2 lb 7 oz**
> **90 g/3½ oz lard**
> **50 g/2 oz olive oil**
> **2 16 cm/6 inch sprigs rosemary**
> **4 fresh sage leaves**
> **2 fresh bay leaves**
> **250 g/8 oz button onions**
> **500 g/1 lb tiny new potatoes, scrubbed**
> **salt and pepper**
> **fistful of fresh parsley, finely chopped**

Joint the lamb (or ask your butcher to do it for you), wash and dry the pieces. Melt the lard and olive oil together in a roasting tin until sizzling, then add the rosemary, sage and bay leaves. Slice half the button onions and add to the herbs. Fry until the onions are soft and translucent, then add the pieces of lamb. Brown on all sides, then add the remaining onions, left whole, and the potatoes. Season generously and place in a cool oven (150°C, 300°F, Gas Mark 2) to roast for 1 hour. Keep an eye on it and move the lamb around, turning over if necessary to prevent sticking. Arrange the lamb, onions, potatoes and sauce on a warmed serving platter, scatter the parsley over the top and serve.

Serves 4

I POLLI · POULTRY AND GAME

POLLO ALLA DIAVOLA · CHICKEN IN THE DEVIL'S STYLE

In the land of witches, wizards, ghosts and demons there has to be a dish that encapsulates all that superstition and mystery. This is a blackened spatchcocked chicken cooked in the minimum amount of time – a really young chicken should take no longer than 20 minutes altogether.

>1 tender poussin
>salt and pepper
>6 sage leaves
>1 bottle Ischia island white wine, or dry white of your choice
>1 tablespoon unsalted butter

Split the bird open and flatten it down to spatchcock it. Heat a wide frying pan and lay the poussin in it, skin side down first. With no fat, brown it quickly on both sides. Season and add the sage leaves, then pour a generous glass of wine over the poussin. When the wine has evaporated rub the butter over the skin of the chicken and cook for a further twenty minutes or until tender. Drink the remaining wine while you cook and eat this delicious chicken dish.

Serves 1

CONIGLIO ALL'ISCHITANA · RABBIT COOKED IN THE ISCHIA STYLE

This is another recipe from the island of Ischia. Almost all the meat dishes of southern Italy include tomatoes in the ingredients.

This deliciously fresh rabbit casserole is no exception. The long cooking time with plenty of moisture makes this a good way of cooking a stringy old jack rabbit.

> 5 tablespoons olive oil
> 1 large rabbit, cut into pieces
> 3 large ripe tomatoes, peeled, deseeded and chopped
> salt and pepper
> 1 large sprig fresh rosemary
> 5 fresh basil leaves
> 1 large glass white wine
> 450 ml/¾ pint water

Heat the olive oil in a deep, heavy-bottomed pan until sizzling. Add the pieces of rabbit and brown them on all sides. Then add the tomatoes, seasoning, rosemary and basil. Cook for about 5 minutes, then pour on the wine. Let the sauce reduce for about 25 minutes, then pour on the water, cover and continue to cook over a medium heat until the meat has absorbed all the water (about 1 hour). It is then ready to serve.

Serves 4–6

I DOLCI · DESSERTS, PIES AND PASTRIES

COVIGLIE AL CAFFE · NEAPOLITAN COFFEE PUDDING

This is a very rich Neapolitan dessert. There really isn't any need to serve more than the tiniest amount. The people of Naples have always been enormously proud of their coffee, so to do this dessert justice make sure the coffee you use is the very best you can obtain.

450 ml/¾ pint milk
1 vanilla pod
200 g/7 oz granulated sugar
5 egg yolks
50 g/2 oz fine plain white flour, sifted
1 coffee cup espresso coffee (about 2–3 tablespoons of
very strong black coffee – not instant)
1 heaped teaspoon powdered coffee
500 ml/17 fl oz whipping cream
24 coffee beans

Pour 1 glass of milk off the 450 ml/¾ pint and set to one side.
Heat the remaining milk to boiling point with the vanilla pod and
the sugar, then remove from the heat. Beat the egg yolks to a
pale-yellow colour with the flour. Add the cold milk, a little at a
time, and then the boiling milk. Never stop whisking or you will
get dreadful lumps in this cream. Finally add the cup of coffee
and then the powdered coffee. Pour this mixture back into the
saucepan where the milk was heated, and let it cool down
completely, stirring gently from time to time to prevent a skin
forming on the surface. When it is cold remove the vanilla pod,
whip 350 ml/12 fl oz of the cream until fairly stiff and fold carefully into the coffee mixture. Then spoon into 12 small bowls or
stemmed glasses and leave in the coldest part of the fridge for
3–4 hours. Whip the rest of the cream and set aside. Just before
serving, decorate each portion with a peaked blob of cream and
2 coffee beans.

Serves 12

COVIGLIE AL CIOCCOLATO · NEAPOLITAN CHOCOLATE PUDDING

Very similar to the coffee version, this is less rich and is normally served with dry biscuits or plain pastries.

> 150 g/5 oz granulated sugar
> 75 g/3 oz unsweetened cocoa powder
> 25 g/1 oz plain white flour
> 500 ml/17 fl oz milk
> 30 g/1¼ oz butter, cut into small cubes
> 400 ml/14 fl oz whipping cream
> 125 g/4 oz candied cherries, chopped

Put the sugar, cocoa powder and flour into a saucepan and mix together. Then add the milk very slowly, stirring gently over a low heat until the mixture boils and thickens slightly. Remove from the heat and stir in the butter, then cool the sauce completely, stirring occasionally to prevent a skin forming on the surface. When it is completely cold, whip two-thirds of the cream and fold in with care. Transfer to a serving dish, individual bowls or stemmed glasses. Chill until required, then whip the rest of the cream until stiff. Decorate the pudding with peaks of cream and scatter the chopped candied cherries over. Serve with dry biscuits or wafers.

Serves 6

PASTIERA NAPOLETANA · NEAPOLITAN EASTER CAKE

This is traditionally served at Easter time. It is really a pie, but the term pie doesn't do it justice. The Campanians are very good at making desserts, and ice creams and pastries are just some of their specialities. This famous Easter cake is well loved all over

Italy and is available in Campanian *pasticcerie* from November to May. This is the time of year when fresh corn is available and Ricotta is supposed to be at its very best. Fresh corn can be bought in pet shops in the UK. To cut down on the preparation time, barley or rice can be substituted for the corn and does not need soaking.

> 250 g/8 oz mais (corn)
> rind of 1 lemon and grated rind of ½ lemon
> 500 ml/17 fl oz milk, boiling hot
> 200 g/7 oz granulated sugar
> pinch of cinnamon
> pinch of salt
> 300 g/10 oz fine plain white flour, sifted
> 9 egg yolks
> 150 g/5 oz lard
> 500 g/1 lb fresh Ricotta cheese
> pinch of mixed spice
> 50 ml/2 fl oz orange flower water
> 90 g/3½ oz candied orange peel, very finely chopped
> 4 egg whites
> butter for greasing
> 5 tablespoons icing sugar, sifted

Cover the corn with cold water and leave to soak for 8 days, changing the water daily. After 8 days, wash and drain the corn and weigh out 250 g/8 oz (it will have swelled and become very much heavier), discarding the rest. Cover the 250 g/8 oz of corn with clean fresh water in a saucepan and bring to the boil. Boil quickly for 15 minutes then strain and put back in the saucepan. Add the whole lemon rind, the boiling hot milk, 1 tablespoon of the sugar, the cinnamon and salt. Simmer covered over the lowest possible heat until the corn has absorbed all the milk – approximately 2 hours. Then remove the lemon rind and pour the corn on to a wide, deep platter to cool.

While the corn is cooking, make the pastry. Put the flour and half the remaining sugar on to the table top, mix together, then blend in 3 of the egg yolks and the lard – knead the pastry only sufficiently to combine all the ingredients. Roll the pastry up into a ball and put in the fridge to chill for at least one hour.

Push the Ricotta through a sieve into a mixing bowl, add the rest of the sugar, a big pinch of mixed spice, the grated lemon rind, the orange flower water and the candied orange peel. Stir in the remaining 6 egg yolks one at a time, being sure that each one is absorbed before the next one is added. Stir in the cold cooked corn. Whisk the egg whites until stiff and fold them into the mixture. Butter a deep 32 cm/13 inch flan tin very thoroughly. Divide the pastry into two pieces, one slightly larger than the other, and roll out. Line the flan tin with the larger piece. Pour in the corn and Ricotta mixture and smooth carefully with a knife. With the remaining piece of pastry make a lattice on top of the flan. Place in a preheated moderate oven (180°C, 350°F, Gas Mark 4) for approximately 1½ hours. Remove the cake from the oven and leave to cool, then dust the surface generously with the sifted icing sugar. Serve directly from the flan tin. This wonderful pie is better if eaten a few days after it has been cooked. It will keep very well in the fridge for up to a week.

Serves 12

PIZZA DOLCE · SWEET PIZZA

This delicious sweet pizza (which is really not very much like the savoury version) can be made with several different fillings. The most common ones are a layer each of homemade black cherry jam and smooth creamy custard, or fresh Ricotta beaten with sugar, egg yolks and lemon rind.

> **325 g/11 oz plain white flour**
> **200 g/7 oz granulated sugar**

4 egg yolks
150 g/5 oz lard, diced
125 g/4 oz sweet almonds, peeled
3 bitter almonds, peeled
1 egg
150 ml/¼ pint milk
½ teaspoon grated lemon rind
200 g/7 oz fresh Ricotta cheese
oil for greasing
flour for dusting
2 tablespoons caster sugar

Make the pastry first. Sift 300 g/10 oz of the flour with 150 g/5 oz of the sugar on to a table top or work surface. Make a hole in the centre with your fist and put 3 egg yolks and the lard into the hole. Knead together until smooth, then wrap in a sheet of oiled greaseproof paper and put in the fridge to chill for at least one hour.

Chop all the almonds very finely together (or use a food processor) and set to one side. Put the remaining 50 g/2 oz sugar, 25 g/1 oz flour and the whole egg into a small saucepan. Whisk until completely combined, then dilute with 125 ml/4 fl oz of the milk. Now place over a very low heat and cook very slowly, stirring constantly until the mixture thickens. Remove from the heat and quickly mix in the remaining egg yolk and the grated lemon rind. Sieve the Ricotta into a bowl, add the custard and the chopped almonds. Stir together very gently so that the mixture stays light and airy. Oil and flour a shallow 30 cm/12 inch cake tin or a deep flan case. Remove the pastry from the fridge and divide it in two, one piece slightly larger than the other. Roll out both pieces and line the cake tin or flan case with the larger one. Pour in the Ricotta filling and smooth carefully with a knife. Lay the second piece of pastry on top of the filling, pinching the edges securely all the way around. Brush with the remaining milk. Place in a preheated warm oven (160°C, 325°F, Gas Mark 3) and bake for 30–40 minutes. Remove from the oven, cool completely and dust with the caster sugar before serving.

Serves 6

ZEPPOLE ISCHITANE · ISCHIA DOUGHNUTS

From Ischia once again come these marvellous little doughnuts with a lovely filling of jam or custard. Traditionally they are made to celebrate St Joseph's Day.

> 150 ml/¼ pint cold water
> pinch of salt
> 30 g/1¼ oz butter, diced
> 90 g/3½ oz fine plain white flour
> 4 egg yolks
> oil for deep frying
> 8–10 tablespoons peach or apricot jam, or thick custard
> 4 tablespoons icing sugar

Heat the water in a saucepan with the salt and butter. As soon as the water boils remove from the heat and sift in the flour, then beat very thoroughly with a wooden spoon. Return to the heat and cook until the mixture comes away from the sides of the saucepan and makes a sizzling sound. Tip it out on to a marble table top or slab and flatten it out with your hands. Leave to cool down, then return to the saucepan. Stir in 1 egg yolk at a time, making sure each one is completely absorbed before adding the next. Wet your hands in cold water and pull off pieces of this dough (about a tablespoon at a time), roll them between your wet hands to produce strips. Coil these round to make 15 small balls. Lay them on an oiled baking tray.

Heat the oil in a deep fryer. When it is sizzling hot, begin to fry the *zeppole* in batches of 4 or 5 at a time until puffy and golden. Lay them in a warmed deep platter on top of a saucepan of simmering water to keep them hot. Split the little doughnuts in half and fill with the jam or custard. Arrange on a platter, sift the icing sugar over, and serve hot.

Makes 15

STRUFFOLI · A CAMPANIAN CHRISTMAS CAKE

Of obvious Arab/Greek/Turkish origin, this incredibly sweet and sticky Christmas cake is about as far as you can get from a traditional Christmas pudding. If you have children, it is the perfect cake to let them 'help you' make in the final stages! They will get horribly sticky but will have a wonderful time.

> 625 g/1 lb 4 oz plain white flour
> pinch of salt
> 1 tablespoon granulated sugar
> grated rind of ½ lemon
> 8 eggs
> 2 egg yolks
> 65 g/2½ oz lard, cut into small pieces
> oil for deep frying
> 250 g/8 oz clear honey
> grated rind of 3 oranges
> 125 g/4 oz candied orange peel, finely chopped
> 125 g/4 oz candied lime peel, finely chopped

Mix together the flour, salt, sugar and lemon rind. Pour out on to the table in a mountain shape, make a hole in the centre and break the eggs into it, then add the yolks and the lard. Knead together very thoroughly to a smooth dough. Divide up and roll out into strips the thickness of your finger. Cut into finger lengths, then cut each length across on the diagonal into approximately 5 rough diamond shapes. Heat the oil in the deep fryer and cook the pieces of dough in batches, scooping them out of the oil with a slotted spoon as soon as they are puffed up, crisp and golden. Drain on kitchen paper.

Put the honey into a saucepan over a medium heat and let it melt. When it is completely runny, remove from the heat and add the grated orange rind. Mix thoroughly, then tip in the fried *struffoli* and the candied peel. Mix together very thoroughly but carefully with a wooden spoon, making sure you don't squash the *struffoli*. When the *struffoli* have absorbed all the honey, tip this mixture out on to a round platter. Wet your hands with cold water and begin to shape the cake by pulling the mixture upwards so it forms a sort of mountain shape. (The modern version is made in a ring mould and this is what you are most likely to be able to buy ready made.) Leave to rest for at least 2 hours before serving.

Serves 8 approximately

LE CONSERVE · PRESERVES

AMARENE AL LIQUORE · BLACK CHERRIES PRESERVED IN THEIR OWN LIQUEUR

These wonderfully juicy, firm black cherries are preserved in liqueur to keep intact all the best flavours of the sunshine and heat. The only thing you really need to make them properly (apart from top-quality cherries) is a whole month of sunshine!

   1 kg/2 lb black cherries
   2 cinnamon sticks

125 g/4 oz granulated sugar
200 ml/7 fl oz white rum
300 ml/½ pint pure alcohol spirit

Wash and dry the cherries thoroughly then tip them into a large storage jar big enough for all the cherries with about 5 cm/ 2 inches headspace (or use 2 separate jars). Add the cinnamon sticks and the sugar. Pour over the rum and mix together. Cover completely with the alcohol spirit and put an airtight lid on the jar. Leave in a sunny place (or somewhere light and warm like on a radiator in a conservatory) for 2 months, shaking up the jar every day to mix it all together. After this time, store the jar in a cool larder or the fridge and use the cherries as required. The liqueur is an excellent *digestif* and the cherries can be added to all kinds of desserts, such as ice cream, fruit salad, etc.

SALSA AL POMODORA · NEAPOLITAN TOMATO SAUCE

In a type of cuisine where the tomato is quite literally put in every dish that isn't a sweet one (at least as far as I know), this extremely quick-to-prepare tomato sauce provides an essential standby. It keeps for up to 6 days in the fridge or can be frozen for up to 4 months.

1 kg/2 lb very soft, ripe tomatoes, washed and quartered
1 large onion, peeled and cut into segments
about 10–12 fresh basil leaves, washed and picked over
large fistful of fresh parsley, washed and picked over

Put all the ingredients into a saucepan, cover and simmer gently for 30 minutes. Put the resulting pulpy mixture through a sieve and transfer to bottles or jars when cool. Keep in the fridge to add to tomato-based sauces and dishes. This is an ideal and very easy way to use up all the overripe and cheap tomatoes that are around at the end of the season.

Makes about 1.5 litres/2½ pints

BOTTIGLIA DI POMODORO · BOTTLED TOMATO SAUCE

In Campania August is the month for preparing this bottled tomato sauce, designed to see any family through the rigours of a bitter winter. Once upon a time entire families would interrupt their summer holidays to spend a couple of days bottling tomatoes for the winter ahead. As a child I remember that the ritual would always take place outdoors, under the shade of a tree, with the bottles wrapped in rags bubbling in great pots hung over a fire of pungent branches. Certainly, tomatoes bottled in this way lose none of their fragrance and flavour, and a plateful of spaghetti dressed simply with a couple of spoonfuls of this sauce and a little olive oil brightens up the snowiest February. The sauce will keep for 4–6 months in a larder or dark cupboard.

> **2 kg/4 lb ripe, firm tomatoes, freshly picked if possible, with absolutely no trace of mould or rot**
>
> **You will also need:**
> **wide-necked, dark glass bottles with corks**
> **a funnel**
> **string**
> **clean rags**
> **large pan in which the bottles can stand upright and be covered in water**

Wash and dry the tomatoes and dunk in boiling water to remove their skins. Then chop coarsely and put into the bottles through a funnel, leaving about 5 cm/2 inches headspace. Cork the bottles very securely, then tie the corks on to the bottles by passing the string under each bottle in a cross shape. Wrap the bottles in thick rags and stand them upright in the pan. Cover all bottles up to the neck with cold water and put on a medium heat. Bring to the boil. From the moment that the water begins to boil, let the tomatoes cook for 20–25 minutes, then remove the pan from the heat. *The water and the tomatoes must be completely cool before you remove the bottles.* Take the *cold* bottles out of the pan, dry them, remove the string and keep them in a larder or dark cupboard to use all winter long.

Makes about 1.5 litres/2½ pints

THE WINES OF CAMPANIA

The wines of this beautiful region with its rich soil full of mineral goodness are lively, warming, cheering and somewhat heady. The further south one travels the stronger the wines become, but in Campania they are still mellow and smooth with fresh, dry flavours predominating.

Here is a list of the best-known favourites:

Aglianico d'Irpinia An intense, ruby-red wine with a smooth, dry flavour made in the Avellino province. It's considered a fine table wine to be drunk with strong-tasting pasta dishes, grilled meats and potent cheeses.

Asprinio A delightful wine that is fast disappearing. It has a lovely greenish-golden tint and is a wine that demands to be drunk very young – within its first year is best. The flavour is fresh and slightly fizzy, and it can be drunk as a table wine or as an aperitif. The best place to find it is probably the town of Aversa and its surroundings.

Capri This very special white wine, produced on the tiny island in very small quantities, is famous throughout the world. A red version also exists but is rarer. The white is pale in colour with a very fragrant bouquet and a fresh, dry flavour. Very good with cold or warm antipasti, fish and shellfish, egg dishes, vegetable dishes and soft cheese.

Falerno Although many think this wine doesn't really belong to Campania and should be considered a wine of the Lazio region I believe it divides up very well into two types, one for Campania and one for Lazio. The Falerno of Campania was the wine preferred by the ancient Romans, as can be deduced from the songs of Horace and Martial and the writings of Pliny the naturalist. The white version is produced exclusively with Falanghina grapes and is straw yellow, with a dry and very slightly bitter flavour. It's perfect with fish, soups and all fried dishes, eggs and Mozzarella. The red version is now produced in tiny quantities as the vineyards are being reconstructed after the earthquake. It's a garnet-coloured wine with a smooth, mellow flavour that can happily be drunk as a good table wine throughout a meal, but is especially fine with stews and roasts.

Fiano This is an aristocratic white wine produced in the Fiano area from grapes also of the same name. It was very much appreciated by the ancient Romans who called it Apianum because the grapes were so loved by bees (the Italian word for bee is *ape*). It's a fresh-tasting, smooth, dry and slightly acidy white wine with a golden straw colour and a very pleasing bouquet.

Gragnano An excellent, rounded and very mellow red wine which improves enormously with age. It has a ruby-to-garnet colour and a distinctive bouquet of violets. It is excellent with strong-tasting cheeses, but can also be enjoyed throughout a meal as a special table wine.

Greco di Tufo An ancient white wine, lauded by Virgil, which is produced in a small area to the north of Avellino. A small part is also turned into spumante. It has a lovely neat, sharp flavour and a wonderful golden colour. A wine to be drunk with all kinds of fish or as a delicious aperitif.

Irpinia Can be red or white. The white version is delicate and fresh tasting, though sometimes it can be fruity, and is very good with white meat and hard cheeses. The red version is dry and well-flavoured and is the very best wine to drink with pizza. This wine is considered to be a summertime drink.

Ischia Bianco A very special and much sought-after white wine produced in various areas of the lovely green island. Very good with seafood, antipasti and light dishes, it has a lovely dry flavour, a straw colouring and a very winy bouquet.

Ischia Rosso This is the red version and is as much sought-after as the white. It's a red that tends towards ruby colour and the wine has an ethereal, delicate bouquet and a very strong, decided flavour. It is very good with *coniglio all'Ischitana*, the local rabbit stew.

Lachryma Christi The name of this almost legendary wine means tears of Christ. It is produced in the area around Vesuvius and appears in both red and white versions. The white can sometimes be a sweet dessert wine. The red is an excellent table wine with all meat dishes while the white is basically a fish wine, though it does tend to be fruity rather than dry.

Ravello Produced all along the famous coastal area of Amalfi, this wine, both red and white, is drunk with all the local fish specialities. In Campania it is quite usual to drink red wine with fish. A good table wine.

Ravello Bianco is an amber-coloured wine with a slightly bitter flavour and is quite alcoholic as table wines go – it can be up to 12.5 degrees proof.

Ravello Rosso is a heavy-coloured ruby wine with an unmistakable bouquet of raspberries. It has a soft and slightly fruity flavour.

Ravello Roseti is the rosé version. It too has a bouquet of raspberries and a very slightly fruity flavour. It's especially good with all fish stews.

Solopaca A wine from the Benevento province which is produced as a red, white or rosé. The white version is intensely straw coloured with a very pleasant bouquet and a dry, pleasing flavour. It is not a white wine to be served chilled. It drinks very well with antipasti and fish or egg dishes but it can also be served as a fine wine to end a meal. The red or rosé versions have a delicate and winy bouquet with a lightly tannic flavour and a lovely velvety characteristic. They are both excellent with roast meats and mature cheeses.

Taurasi Another wine which was much appreciated by the ancient Romans, it is produced in the province of Avellino. It has been nicknamed the Barbaresco of the South. It has a heavy ruby colouring, a very pleasing bouquet, and a light and harmoniously dry and aromatic flavour. It is a special wine to be drunk with red meat, game dishes, mature cheeses and other very special dishes.

Vesuvio Produced at the feet of the famous volcano in two versions, Vesuvio Bianco which has a very pale colour, a bouquet of violets, a slightly fizzy flavour and is a table wine that marries especially well with fish, and the less characteristic red version: Vesuvio Rosso which has many of the same virtues but is a red wine that does not age well and must be drunk young.

Other wines of the region include:
In the province of Avellino: Paterno and San Giorgio.
In the province of Benevento: Pannarano and Vitulano.
In the province of Caserta: Conca.
In the province of Naples: Bianco di Procida and Monte Procida.
In the province of Salerno: Cilento Rosso, Alto Cilento, Corbara, Irno Rosso, Irno Bianco and Tramonti.

· APULIA ·

Apulia is known as 'the Lombardy of the South' because of its industrial and commercial activities. These make it one of the most successful of the southern regions, if not the most successful. The super-efficient ports and the almost perfect flatness of the landscape have made it possible to build and develop, especially in the areas around Taranto, Bari and Brindisi. Here you'll find Italy's most important steelworks, vast oil refineries, the country's largest salt fields, and multiple plastic and chemical factories – all contrasting very sharply with Apulia's ancient and established traditions of fishing, agriculture, wine and oil making, pasta, tobacco, jam and conserve industries.

However, it wasn't always like this down here. For hundreds of years lack of water made the quality of life almost unbearable for the many inhabitants of the region. Nineteen centuries ago Caesar planned an aqueduct bringing water from the River Sele in Irpinia to this thirsty land. But the work was only finally begun in 1906 and, after many years of immense effort and superhuman tribulation, water has finally reached these homes, fields and industries, even if it still isn't always enough. In Apulia it only rains in the winter months, and then only very little.

Since the water came, the population has grown as the need for immigration to the rich north has lessened. Water is still a problem; a bigger supply would mean that production of Apulia's fantastic variety of fruit and vegetables, wine, oil and nuts would double, and that many of the sterile, uncultivated areas could flourish. However, Italy tends to forget the problems of the south, and despite Apulia's commercial success there are still parts of this region that feel light years away from the decision-making powers of Rome.

Apulia is perhaps the least 'Italian' of all the southern regions. From neighbouring Greece it has taken its colours, flavours, style and scents. This may be 'southern Lombardy', but at heart it is the land of shepherds and fishermen, of almond trees, olive groves and vineyards that need little moisture, and of a basic simplicity of life.

As elsewhere in the south, isolated farms and houses are a rarity. Peasants and farmers live in large villages and rural townships; when one is poor there is wisdom in numbers. Four-tenths of the population live in the province of Bari, the main city.

Like all Italy's regions, Apulia is divided up into provinces, but it is really four separate areas rather than five provinces. These are: the Gargano, the Tavoliere, the Murghe and the Penisola Salentina. It is almost as though the natural layout of the land-scape has obstinately overridden the official denominations.

The loveliness of Apulia is little appreciated by the rest of the country, with the exception of the Gargano, which is a very popular holiday resort. The spur of the boot, it forms a promon-tory with cliffs and white beaches to the south and rolling slopes and lagoons to the north. At the centre is the dense forest of pines, oaks, elms and beeches known as la foresta Umbra.

The Tavoliere is Italy's largest peninsular plain. Blessed by the natural water resources of the two rivers that border it, it tends to be boggy in parts. It is a natural area for pastureland, and during Greek, Roman and Byzantine rule it was always used for this purpose. Nowadays it is intensely cultivated, yielding a rich abundance of crops, including wheat, and only part of it is still used as pasture.

The Murghe lies to the south of the Tavoliere, forming a calcareous area rather like a low, flat plain, which slopes away to the coastline. Here, the underground water resources that would be so valuable to this region are suddenly visible. Here and there, water gushes to the surface for a while only to disappear and return to the surface again in the very fertile band running parallel to the coast, known as La Terra di Bari. You would think it should solve all their problems if only these existing natural water sources could be used, but that would be just too easy! All that needs to happen, in theory, is that wells are dug for the water to be reached, and over the years many peasants have done just that. But now the resources have dwin-dled dramatically and salt water has invaded the underwater streams – killing off just the crops it is used to quench.

The Penisola Salentina lies to the south of the Murghe, stretching down to the cape of Santa Maria di Leuca, the point of the heel. It is a long, flat plain sandwiched between the Adriatic and Ionian seas with a small group of hills at the very south. Here the surface of the soil is arid and dry, but underground run many streams and bubbling springs. In ancient times this long peninsula was called Calabria, as it was part of that region. Yet it is here that the Greek influence is most vivid and tangible; to many it is still known as *le terre Greche* (the Greek lands). This peninsula is where Apulia's exceptional vegetables grow best.

These four areas are divided into the provinces of Bari, Brindisi, Foggia, Lecce and Taranto. Although Bari is Apulia's main city it doesn't dominate the style and culture of the region as Naples does in Campania. Each of the five cities has its own character, and the provinces reflect this.

Bari is a bustling port with an old city full of narrow, winding, cobbled alleys and tiny squares, in complete contrast to the massive modern port buildings and endless quays. Within the province is the little town of Bitonto, its perfect olive oil so famous that many local recipes actually specify its use. Alberobello is the place to visit if you want to see Apulia's most famous landmarks, the *trulli*, curious little conical-shaped buildings that have been built here for centuries. Made from lumps of local stone they have many uses – storage, animal shelter, habitation – and are a real flight of architectural fantasy. The oddest thing is seeing them in the suburbs of modern, apartment-block townships. Within walking distance of an eight-storey building you can find a group of these primitive, very low, white buildings with their pointed roofs and tiny little windows to keep out the unrelenting heat.

Brindisi, where the ferries from Greece dock and load up, is second in order of importance. The busy city sprawls untidily around the old town centre with a very ugly collection of industrial sites, which have risen upwards and outwards ever since the vast ships bearing crude oil began to join the throngs of holiday-makers.

Foggia and her province lie across the Tavoliere. Horribly bombed during the war, the city still has an air of post-war recovery to this day. Before the war it was one of the most important livestock centres of the south, and shepherds and cowherds used to walk from Campania and the Abruzzi to gather at Foggia market. Nowadays it is principally an agricultural town, dealing with the crops yielded by the Tavoliere. Within this province lie the delightful archipelago of islands called Le Tremiti – four perfect holiday spots for those who can get there.

To my mind Lecce has to be the loveliest of Apulia's cities, and one of the prettiest in the entire south. Judging by the wealth of architectural heritage on view, its golden era was the sixteenth and seventeenth centuries. Mostly built out of the glorious *pietra Leccese*, everything is deliciously ochre tinged, with a deep warm hue. Surrounding the city is a province made up of vast olive groves and vineyards, small villages and townships and very beautiful coastline. In part of the province of Otranto which lies exactly opposite the Albanian coast, surprisingly there are still local Albanian settlements where Albanian is spoken, and where the people have stuck to their religions (some of them are Moslems), traditions and culture, completely ignoring the fact that they are living in Italy. In some of the settlements they continue to wear Albanian national costume as a matter of course.

After Bari, Taranto is the most densely inhabited of the five cities. It lies on the Ionian coast in a very unusual position. The original Greek settlement was built on a thin strip of sand in between two bays called Mar Piccolo and Mar Grande, and it is here that the heart of the city still beats. The modern city, with its frenetic traffic system, has mostly been built to the east, between the two stretches of sea. The narrow strip of land is crisscrossed by two canals, and it is because of its excellent defensive position that the city has been chosen as base and arsenal for the Italian navy. The industrial development of Taranto as a steelworks centre and refinery port has caused immeasurable damage. The sky has lost its healthy, sunny glow, there is a very serious air and sea pollution problem, and the almost overnight success of the area has resulted in a succession of disastrous and badly planned building programmes. The province spreads across the Murghe into the Salentina, with Martina Franca as its major centre. This town lies in a delightful fertile area of vineyards growing the delicious Uva Regina grape and dotted with *trulli*. Taranto itself is a main centre for the cultivation of oysters and mussels. Huge beds producing these marvellous fruits of the sea are very carefully controlled since the last cholera epidemic in the early 1970s.

Just like Greek cuisine, the dishes of Apulia make the most of what is available locally. The meat is almost always mutton, lamb or kid. Very rarely horse meat appears on the menu, and although beef, poultry and pork have recently invaded the kitchens of Apulia they are not part of the traditional cuisine of this ancient land. The cheeses have the flavour and intensity of ewe's milk; the olive oil is rich, green-gold and smooth, as it has been for many centuries; the fruit and vegetables are bursting with sweet sunshine; there is golden honey with which to make pastries and puddings, an abundance of herbs, and olives in every shade of black and green.

Very popular locally, but quite definitely an acquired taste, are the wild onions called *lampascioni*, or *lampasciuli*. They taste unique, very bitter and onion/garlicky, strange to say the least. But the real symbol of the cuisine of Apulia is without a shadow of a doubt the tiny, round, dark-red, firm, sweet and juicy tomato. Tomatoes like this don't grow anywhere else, and their flavour is a completely new experience. You'll find them in salads and stews, on the local version of pizza, but above all on the delicious local pasta.

There are just two basic shapes of pasta in Apulia, both traditionally handmade with expertise, knowledge and artistry. A thick dough is used, which creates a much more substantial mouthful than the elegant tagliatelle of the north. The most popular of the two is orecchiette (little ears), so called because they look like small animal ears. The dough is rolled out like a snake, then sliced into discs. Each disc is pushed and drawn across a coarse table top to make it concave and lined, so that it will absorb and scoop up as much sauce as possible once dressed.

The other shape is called cavatieddi and is a smaller version of orecchiette, except that the end result looks more like little seashells. Egg is not used in the local, handmade pasta, just a mixture of coarse flour, semolina and water. The pasta is dried until brittle and hard, and therefore requires quite a long cooking time.

Herbs are an integral part of all Apulian dishes, and rue, marjoram, thyme, oregano and bay are used in many local specialities. Undoubtedly, this is one of the healthiest cuisines in the world, where simple flavours and excellent raw materials are put together with traditional skill.

In Apulia, simplicity is always the most important consideration when it comes to food. This cuisine takes the very best and most natural local ingredients and turns them into dishes that are rustic, unfussy and delicious, low in saturated fats and rich in all the good things the countryside and the sea have to offer. Not for Apulia the wild, baroque extravagances of Sicilian cooking, nor the exuberant colours of Campanian cuisine; yet there is a wealth of flair and imagination in these kitchens, a marvellous combination of tradition, innovation and skill. The end results are nothing short of magical; try a succulent lamb casserole from which the sauce is drawn and used to dress orecchiette as a filling first course, then the meat served with perfect vegetables as a second course, and honey-drenched pastries to round off a perfect meal. One-pot cooking, born out of sheer necessity, is still very much in use here.

Apulia, unsurprisingly considering the 706 kilometres of coastline that surround it, provides Italy with most of its fish and seafood. All manner of fresh fish is available in Apulia, from lobsters, shrimps, prawns and squid to mackerel, sea bass and mullet. Many of the fish have local names that change from one province to another, so don't be surprised if the fish you see in the market at Bari has a different name when you see it again in Brindisi. Particularly good are the delicious dishes of tender octopus or squid, and especially memorable is the superb *polpi sott'aceto* (pickled octopus).

The preserved and cured meats of this area tend to be very lean and dry, quite different from those in next-door Calabria or further to the north. The salami are small, hard and compact, very dark red in colour and strong and pungent in flavour.

There is an infinite variety of delicious cheeses, ranging from buffalo-milk Mozzarella, pure white Ricotta, which is used extensively in desserts and cakes, smoked cheeses, buttery cheeses, and fresh cheeses floating in whey. No Parmesan, of course; this is replaced by Pecorino, a hard grating cheese, or breadcrumbs fried until crisp in olive oil. Pecorino is more or less strong tasting and smelling depending upon its degree of maturity.

Fish and vegetable dishes, along with pies, pizzas and flans of various kinds, take preference over meat dishes, which is just the kind of food that appeals the most in such hot weather. Remember it never really gets cold here, and it only ever rains in the winter, so there is no need for the kind of food that warms and sticks to the ribs!

Daunia is the ancient Greek name given to the area that nowadays corresponds approximately to the province of Foggia. I keep coming across recipes with the subtitle 'speciality of the Daunian cuisine', so I like to imagine the inhabitants of these parts as great gourmets of times long gone. Certainly, the Daunian specialities are absolutely delicious and it is obvious why they have passed the test of time.

I always leave the warmth and loveliness of this relatively unspoilt region with a heavy heart. One more excursion to catch lunch in these transparent blue waters, one more plateful of orecchiette, one more dinner of succulent lamb cooked on a spit over a pungently scented fire of fresh herbs and wood, one more erotic – almost obscenely ripe – pink fig, one more slice of juicy,

brilliant-orange melon, just one last jug of ice-cold white wine
. . . I always dawdle, dreaming of making my home right here
with these quiet people who are 'careful' at first, then open to
friendship, ready to share what little they have with those they
like and trust, in an olive grove with *trulli* in the distance, waves
lapping at the foot of the cliff and almond blossom at my
window . . .

My favourite moment in my beloved Apulia? It must be the
insight I was given into the wonderfully eccentric mind of
Emperor Frederick II, grandson of the infamous Barbarossa and,
according to many historians, one of the most brilliant monarchs
of the Middle Ages.

This quintessential Mediterranean man, brought up in Sicily by
several tutors after the death of his parents, grew up speaking six
languages and fired by a passionate love for southern Italy. He
became Holy Roman Emperor quite by accident when the right-
ful heir, Otto of Brunswick, was defeated by the French at the
battle of Bouvines in 1215. Frederick spent much of his reign
trying to tie up his properties in the north with those in the south,
and was always in the midst of arguments with his sons, the Holy
See or the Guelf Pope supporters, in some part of Italy. However,
he also found time to make many contributions to the arts,
commissioning churches, palaces, castles and other buildings.
Under his guidance and patronage, sculptors, artists and, in
particular, architects contributed to a classical revival, as can be
seen in friezes, archways and triumphant medieval architecture
all over southern Italy. My all-time favourite is the honey-
coloured castle at Astel del Monte, near Andria. It is quite
mysterious as it has almost no windows whatsoever and absolutely no kitchens or living quarters for servants. Maybe he
always ate out . . . ?

LE MINESTRE · SOUP

MINESTRA MARITATA · LAYERED SOUP

This is an ancient speciality of the Daunian civilization. Daunia was the name the ancient Greeks gave to the area that more or less corresponds to the province of Foggia. Apulia is rightfully famous throughout Italy for its wonderful soups and first courses.

    1 kg/2 lb Batavian endive (escarole)
    1 kg/2 lb sweet chicory
    500 g/1 lb celery hearts
    500 g/1 lb fennel
    125 g/4 oz lard
    1 litre/1¾ pints meat stock (or strong-flavoured
    vegetable stock)
    125 g/4 oz Pecorino cheese, freshly grated
    freshly ground black pepper
    oil for greasing

Clean and pick over all the vegetables and cook separately in salted water until just tender. Drain and set aside in separate containers. Chop up the lard and mix it with the meat or vegetable stock. Bring to the boil and simmer for 15 minutes. Grease a casserole lightly and arrange the vegetables in it in separate layers. Cover each layer with a little stock, a generous sprinkling of cheese and a good grinding of black pepper. Put the layered soup over a moderate heat and cook through for an extra 15 minutes. Remove from the heat and allow to rest for 40 minutes before serving. Serve lukewarm.

Serves 6

MINESTRA IN BRODO DI PESCE · FISH STOCK SOUP

From the town of Bitonto comes this delicious soup which calls specifically for the fabulous oil of that town if possible. It is a very fresh-tasting soup of whiting, tomatoes, garlic, oil and parsley boiled together, then the fish is removed and served as the second course, while pasta is cooked in the fish broth and served as the first course.

> **large fistful of fresh parsley, coarsely chopped**
> **1 large clove garlic, peeled and sliced into strips**
> **3 large ripe tomatoes, skinned, chopped and deseeded**
> **5 tablespoons olive oil**
> **salt and pepper**
> **1 small whiting, weighing approximately 700 g/1 lb 7 oz, cleaned and gutted**
> **200 g/7 oz small macaroni**
> **juice of 1 lemon**

Put the parsley, garlic and tomatoes into a pan with the olive oil, add enough water to make soup for 4 (approximately 750 ml/1¼ pints) and season with salt and pepper. Bring to the boil and simmer for about 10 minutes then add the whiting. Cook for about 7 minutes then lift the fish out and tip in the pasta. When the pasta is ready the soup is served and the whiting makes up the second course of the meal with a generous squeeze of lemon juice.

Serves 4

MINESTRA DI FAVE E CARCIOFI · BROAD BEAN AND ARTICHOKE SOUP

This delicious combination of globe artichokes and broad beans in a superb soup comes from the beautiful city of Lecce.

> 1.5 kg/3 lb fresh broad beans (unshelled weight)
> 6 globe artichokes
> 1 lemon, sliced
> 250 g/8 oz onions, coarsely chopped
> 1 celery stick, coarsely chopped
> 125 ml/4 fl oz olive oil
> salt and pepper

Shell the beans and put them in a basin of cold water to soak. Clean the artichokes and cut them into quarters, then, to prevent them discolouring, put them in a basin of cold water containing the lemon slices. Put the onions and celery into a pot with the olive oil, then drain the beans and artichokes and add to the pot. Add a generous 1 litre/1¾ pints cold water, season with salt and pepper and bring to the boil. Simmer under a lid until the vegetables begin to fall apart, then serve very hot.

Serves 4

PASTA · PASTA

ORECCHIETTE CON CIME DI RAPA · ORECCHIETTE WITH TURNIP TOPS

Orecchiette are Apulia's little ears, the traditional pasta shape that they make so carefully in these parts and have done for many generations. This is the most typical of all Apulia's pasta recipes.

> **125 g/4 oz semolina**
> **250 g/8 oz plain white flour**
> **pinch of salt**
> **about 6 tablespoons warm water**
> **400 g/13 oz turnip tops, washed and coarsely chopped**
> **8 tablespoons olive oil**
> **freshly ground black pepper**

Mix the semolina and flour together with the salt and enough warm water to make a dough about the same consistency as bread dough. If anything make it slightly stiffer. Roll out into sausage shapes about 10 cm/4 inches long. Cut off tiny discs from the dough with a very sharp knife, then using the tip of the knife run each disc across a rough surface to make it concave. Then put the piece of pasta on the end of your thumb and press it down and across to make a little ear shape. They should be approximately 3 cm/1½ inches diameter and fairly thick. Orecchiette can be bought ready made, but if you do make your own they must be left to dry in the open air for at least 4 hours, until they are completely hard. They are the most traditional symbol of the cuisine of Apulia.

Cook the dried orecchiette and turnip tops together in plenty of boiling salted water, adding the turnip tops about 6 minutes after the pasta. The pasta will take about 20 minutes to cook. Drain carefully, dress with plenty of good rich olive oil and black pepper, toss together and serve at once.

Serves 4

PASTA AI PEPERONI · PASTA WITH SWEET PEPPERS

The peppers of the south are magnificent, and in this recipe they are combined with little macaroni for a very traditional Apulian theme of pasta and vegetables. In this case the effect is especially magical thanks to the marriage of tomato and peppers. Obviously the fresher and better the raw ingredients are, the better the finished dish will taste and look.

> 500 g/1 lb red, yellow or green peppers, or a mixture
> 85 ml/3 fl oz olive oil
> salt and pepper
> 500 g/1 lb fresh ripe tomatoes, or use equivalent canned or passata
> 50 g/2 oz fresh parsley, chopped
> 2 cloves garlic, finely chopped
> 400 g/13 oz maccheroncini rigati (small, lined macaroni), or other smallish, stubby pasta
> 3 heaped tablespoons grated Pecorino cheese

Wash and dry the peppers, then, holding them on a fork, char them quickly over a flame (a candle will do) until the outer skin is completely blistered and loosened. Plunge the peppers into cold water and rub off the outer skin with a dry cloth. Cut them open, remove all the seeds and inner membrane and slice them lengthways into neat, even strips. Heat the oil in a deep pan, add the peppers, season and cook through quickly on a lively heat; do not let them go mushy. As soon as the peppers are cooked, remove from the pan and put aside on a plate. If using fresh tomatoes, cut into quarters and add to the pan in which the peppers were cooked. Season and add the parsley and garlic. Lower the heat and simmer gently.

Meanwhile, bring a large pot of salted water to the boil, then throw in the pasta and stir. Five minutes before the pasta is cooked, add the peppers to the tomatoes. Drain the pasta, dress with the pepper and tomato mixture, cover with the cheese and serve at once.

Serves 4

VERMICELLI CON LA MOLLICA · VERMICELLI WITH BREADCRUMBS

Another speciality from Bitonto, where fried breadcrumbs are used in place of cheese. This is common practice amongst those poor households that cannot afford to buy Pecorino or Parmesan to grate over their pasta. The bright-emerald-green Apulian cauliflower is also often served with fried breadcrumbs in this way – a local interpretation of cauliflower cheese!

    1 onion, finely chopped
    1 celery stick, finely chopped
    5 anchovy fillets, finely chopped
    8 tablespoons olive oil
    400 g/13 oz fresh ripe tomatoes, quartered, or use
    equivalent canned or passata
    salt and pepper
    325 g/11 oz vermicelli (thin spaghetti)
    50 g/2 oz fresh breadcrumbs

Fry the onion, celery, anchovy fillets in half the olive oil until the onion is translucent. Add the tomatoes, season, cover and simmer for 30 minutes on a very low heat. Bring a pot of salted water to a fast boil, throw in the vermicelli, stir and cook until *al dente*. Meanwhile, heat the rest of the oil and fry the breadcrumbs in it until golden and crisp. Drain the pasta, dress with the tomato sauce and cover with the fried breadcrumbs before serving.

Serves 4

PASTA E BROCCOLI · PASTA WITH BROCCOLI

In this case the broccoli called for are the little 'calabrese' as sold in the UK. You need only the florets, no leaves or hard stalks. It is a very full-flavoured dish that really shouts about its origins.

1.2 kg/2 lb 7 oz sprouting broccoli
300 g/10 oz penne or bucatini (or other thickish, tubular pasta)
6 tablespoons olive oil
1 clove garlic
½ dried red chilli
50 g/2 oz anchovy fillets
salt

Remove all the leaves from the broccoli and cut off any hard stems so that you end up with just the florets and all the tender pieces. Toss into a pot of boiling salted water and cook until tender. Remove from the pot with a slotted spoon and keep warm. Cook the pasta in the same water as the broccoli. Meanwhile heat the oil in a pan with the garlic and chilli. Remove the garlic and chilli as soon as the garlic is browned. Add the anchovy fillets, mash them into the oil until creamy, and keep hot. When the pasta is cooked, drain it and add to the broccoli. Toss together and dress with the flavoured oil. Serve immediately.

Serves 4

PIZZA · PIZZA

CALSUNCIEDDI · LITTLE FRIED PIZZAS

Pies, pizza and pasties are very much a part of the local cuisine. These are little deep-fried pockets of pizza dough stuffed with cheese and ham, and are similar to the Campanian *calzoni*.

FOR THE DOUGH
400 g/13 oz plain white flour
25 g/1 oz fresh yeast, diluted in 2 tablespoons warm water
1 tablespoon olive oil
salt

FOR THE FILLING
300 g/10 oz Mozzarella cheese, chopped
200 g/7 oz fresh Ricotta cheese
200 g/7 oz ham, chopped
125 g/4 oz Caciocavallo cheese, diced (or use very mature Cheddar)
2 eggs, beaten
3 tablespoons olive oil
½ teaspoon sugar
salt

Mix the flour, yeast, water, olive oil and salt together to a smooth dough. Knead thoroughly for about 10 minutes, then leave in a warm place until doubled in size. Roll out as thinly as possible and cut into 12 cm/4½ inch circles. Lay them out on a floured tray and leave in a warm place to rise for another hour. Meanwhile put all the ingredients for the filling into a bowl and mix together. Spoon a little filling into the centre of half of each circle of dough, fold the empty half of the circle over it in such a way that a flap is left sticking out. Fold this back over the join and press it down all the way round the half circle with the prongs of a fork. Deep fry until crisp and golden, drain on kitchen paper, sprinkle with salt and serve.

Makes about 22; serves about 6

PIZZA DI VERDURA · RADICCHIO PIZZA

This is really more of a pie than a pizza, though it uses pizza dough rather than pastry. However, like a pie, the filling of radicchio, capers, olives and garlic is on the inside. Perfect for cold buffets and picnics, it's a marvellous way of using radicchio.

> 400 g/13 oz plain white flour
> pinch of salt
> pinch of white pepper
> 30 g/1¼ oz fresh yeast, diluted in a little warm water
> 1.2 kg/2 lb 7 oz radicchio, washed and coarsely chopped
> 4 tablespoons olive oil
> 1 clove garlic, peeled
> salt and pepper
> 50 g/2 oz capers, washed, squeezed dry, then chopped
> 50 g/2 oz black olives, stoned
> 1 egg, beaten

Put the flour on to the table top in a hill shape. Make a hole in the centre with your closed fist and put the salt, white pepper and yeast in the hole. Mix into the flour, then add enough warm water to knead the dough to a smooth ball. Knead for about 10 minutes, then leave in a warm place to rise for about 2 hours or until doubled in size.

Put the radicchio in a frying pan with the oil and garlic. Season, cover, then cook gently over a low heat until tender. When the dough has risen, divide it into two pieces. Roll out one piece as thinly as possible to cover the bottom and sides of a 23 cm/9 inch cake or pie tin. Fill with the cooked radicchio, the capers and the olives. Roll out the second piece of dough and cover the 'pizza' with it. Seal the edges carefully by pinching together with your fingertips. Brush the top with the beaten egg and bake in a preheated moderate oven (180°C, 350°F, Gas Mark 4) for 30 minutes. Serve cold.

Serves 6–8

IL RISO · RICE

TIELLA DI RISO E COZZE · RICE AND MUSSELS

Unusually for the area, this recipe, a speciality of the city of Bari, contains rice. It is a layered dish of rice, potatoes and the wonderful local mussels, dressed with tomatoes, onions, Pecorino, garlic, parsley and the very best olive oil. A real triumph of a dish that is served cold as part of a buffet.

> **fistful of fresh parsley, washed**
> **2 cloves garlic, peeled**
> **500 g/1 lb fresh mussels**
> **2 large onions, thinly sliced into rings**
> **500 g/1 lb fresh ripe tomatoes, coarsely chopped, or use equivalent canned drained tomatoes**
> **6 level tablespoons grated Pecorino cheese**
> **salt and pepper**
> **500 g/1 lb potatoes, peeled and sliced to 0.5 cm/¼ inch thickness**
> **300 g/10 oz long grain rice, washed and drained**

8 tablespoons olive oil
750 ml/1¼ pints cold water

Chop the parsley with the garlic and set aside. Scrub and de-beard the mussels, wash very carefully, then prise open with the point of a sharp knife. Throw away the empty shells and set the mussels aside. Sprinkle a layer of onion rings in the bottom of a deep, oiled roasting tin. Spread over it half of the chopped parsley and garlic, then half the tomatoes, and cover with all the Pecorino. Season, then cover with a layer of potatoes and spread the wet rice over. Arrange the open mussels on the rice, scatter the remaining chopped parsley, onion and garlic over, cover with the remaining tomatoes, and finish off with the remaining potatoes. Pour the oil over the dish and then pour the water in. Place in a preheated moderate oven (180°C, 350°F, Gas Mark 4) for about 30 minutes or until the rice is completely cooked. Allow to cool down almost completely before serving.

Serves 6

I LEGUMI · VEGETABLES

INVOLTINI DI PEPERONI · STUFFED PEPPERS

Another speciality of the Daunian cuisine, these are juicy yellow peppers stuffed with breadcrumbs, capers, pine kernels, sultanas, anchovies and parsley, baked with olive oil until just soft.

1 tablespoon sultanas
2 very large yellow peppers, or 4 small ones
1 tablespoon capers, washed and chopped

2 salted or canned anchovies, cleaned, boned and
chopped
4 tablespoons pine kernels
1 tablespoon chopped fresh parsley
4 tablespoons fresh white breadcrumbs
7 tablespoons olive oil (more if necessary)
salt and pepper

Soak the sultanas in warm water for 15 minutes then drain and
dry them. Char the peppers over a flame so that the skin blisters
all over, then plunge them into cold water and rub the skin off
with a dry cloth. Cut them open lengthways and remove the seeds
and white membranes. Put the capers and anchovies into a bowl
and add the pine kernels, sultanas, parsley and breadcrumbs.
Add enough oil to mix to a smooth paste, season and spoon into
the pepper halves. Place in an oiled ovenproof dish, sprinkle
with olive oil and bake in a preheated moderate oven (180°C,
350°F, Gas Mark 4) for 15–20 minutes. Serve hot or cold.

Serves 4

INSALATA DI MELANZANE ALLA GRIGLIA · GRILLED AUBERGINE SALAD

This superb salad of grilled, cold aubergines comes from Lecce.
It sounds very odd, I know, but it is really delicious and the
generous sprinkling of vinegar takes away all the sweet, cloying
flavour that grilled aubergines can have.

2 very large, preferably oval aubergines
4 tablespoons olive oil
1 clove garlic, finely chopped
salt and pepper
a little best-quality wine vinegar

Heat the grill. Remove the stalks from the aubergines and cut them into thickish slices lengthways. Brush each slice with olive oil mixed with the chopped garlic, salt and pepper. Grill for about 4 minutes on each side or until cooked through. Allow to cool completely, then sprinkle a little vinegar over and serve as a side salad.

Serves 4

MAZZETTI DI ASPARAGI FRITTI · FRIED ASPARAGUS BUNCHES

This is one of those Daunian cuisine specialities. The original recipe calls for wild asparagus but sprue will work equally well.

> **500 g/1 lb sprue or wild asparagus, trimmed and washed**
> **flour**
> **2 eggs, beaten**
> **salt**
> **oil for deep-frying**
> **lemon wedges**

Boil the asparagus or sprue until tender, then drain and secure into small bunches (8 bunches if possible). Dip the bunches first in flour, then into the beaten eggs with a little salt added. Deep fry in hot oil until crisp and golden – about 4 minutes. Drain and serve immediately with lemon wedges.

Serves 4

PEPERONI SOFFRITTI CON LE UOVA · SCRAMBLED EGGS WITH TOMATOES AND PEPPERS

Another speciality of the Daunia is this delicious combination of creamily scrambled eggs with sweet peppers. This dish is traditionally served as an accompaniment, but when peppers are at their best I like to serve it as a light lunch or supper dish.

>500 g/1 lb peppers
>2–3 fresh ripe tomatoes, chopped, or use equivalent canned and drained tomatoes
>4 tablespoons olive oil
>salt
>2 large eggs, beaten

Wash and dry the peppers, then cut into neat strips, removing all seeds and white membranes. Fry the peppers gently with the tomatoes in the olive oil until soft and cooked through but not mushy. Beat a pinch of salt into the eggs and pour them over the peppers and tomatoes. Lower the heat and very slowly scramble the eggs with the vegetables – you are not making an omelette. Serve as soon as the eggs are lightly set.

Serves 4

I PESCI · FISH

COZZE RIPIENE AL SUGO · STUFFED DRESSED MUSSELS

This is a deliciously intricate dish, with the stuffed mussels tied up with string to secure the filling. It takes a certain amount of skill and patience to prepare but the effort is well worth it. However, it's not the sort of thing to tackle if you're in a hurry. A marvellous way of making the most of really good fresh mussels.

1 kg/2 lb fresh mussels
2 cloves garlic
4 tablespoons olive oil
250 g/8 oz passata
6 fresh basil leaves, slightly bruised
salt
150 ml/¼ pint cold water
2 eggs, beaten
fistful of fresh parsley, finely chopped
3 tablespoons very fine fresh breadcrumbs

Wash and scrub the mussels with great care. Using a sharp knife, prise the shells open just enough to allow the mussels to open out but leaving them attached to both shells. Wash in lightly salted water and set aside. Peel 1 clove of garlic and fry in the oil until brown, then remove and discard. Add the passata, basil leaves and salt to the oil, and simmer for about 5 minutes, then add the water. Stir, cover, and leave to cook gently.

Peel and finely chop the remaining clove of garlic and mix with the eggs, parsley and breadcrumbs. Use a little of this mixture to fill each opened mussel. Tie up the mussels with white thread to keep the stuffing in place. Put them in the saucepan with the tomato sauce and cover. Cook gently for about 20 minutes and remove the thread before serving. If there is enough sauce, use it to dress some plain boiled rice to serve with the mussels.

Serves 4

SEPPIE RIPIENE · STUFFED SQUID

4 large squid
6 tablespoons olive oil
2 cloves garlic
8 fresh ripe tomatoes, chopped, or use equivalent
canned, drained tomatoes
salt and pepper
water or fish stock to cover
1 egg, beaten
3 level tablespoons fresh breadcrumbs
3 level tablespoons grated Pecorino cheese
fistful of fresh parsley, chopped

Clean the squid carefully inside and out. Remove the thin outer layer of skin, then push your finger inside it and turn the sac inside out; remove the inner skin and wash off all the dirt that collects inside. Remove the tentacles, wash and chop them, then put them aside. Heat 5 tablespoons of the oil in a pan with 1 clove of garlic, peeled but left whole. When the garlic is browned remove and discard it, then add the tomatoes. Season, cover and leave to simmer for about 30 minutes. Add enough water or fish stock to the tomato sauce during the cooking to ensure it will cover all the squid when you put them in the pan.

Now make the stuffing. Chop the remaining garlic clove and mix with the chopped tentacles, the egg, breadcrumbs, Pecorino, parsley, and the remaining tablespoon of olive oil. Stuff the 4 squid with this mixture, and sew them up with white thread. Gently lower each one into the tomato sauce and cover. Cook for about 20 minutes or until tender. Remove the thread before serving.

Serves 4

TRIGLIA AL CARTOCCIO · PAPER-BAKED RED MULLET

This method of baking fish in paper is used all over Italy. Here is the Apulian version which relies very heavily on the dressing of the fish, using herbs, olives, oil, and no lemon juice as in other versions. Naturally the red mullet must be as fresh and perfect as possible.

> **4 medium-sized red mullet**
> **salt and pepper**
> **dried oregano**
> **olive oil**
> **chopped fresh parsley**
> **16 black olives**

Scrape and clean the red mullet, wash them carefully and lay each one in the centre of a square of oiled baking parchment. Season with salt, pepper and oregano, both inside and out. Sprinkle with olive oil and chopped parsley and place 4 olives on the back of each fish. Wrap them up in the parchment and put in a roasting tin. Place the tin in a preheated hot oven (220°C, 425°F, Gas Mark 7) for about 15 minutes, turning the parcels over halfway through the cooking time. Serve wrapped up so each person has the pleasure of unwrapping their own fish.

Serves 4

LE CARNI · MEAT

U'VERDETTE · ROAST LAMB WITH EGG AND CHEESE

Despite its strange name, which roughly translated means 'the greenery', this is actually a roast lamb dish! In Bari it's an Easter speciality, a lovely combination of lamb, fresh peas and onions cooked together, then finished off with eggs, parsley and Pecorino cheese to form a thick sauce around the meat.

    1 shoulder or leg of lamb, boned, weighing
    approximately 800 g/1 lb 10 oz
    1 large onion, sliced
    6 tablespoons olive oil
    1 glass dry white wine
    500 g/1 lb fresh peas, shelled
    2 large eggs, beaten
    5 tablespoons grated Pecorino cheese
    pinch of salt
    fistful of fresh parsley, coarsely chopped

Cube the meat. Fry the onion briefly in the oil in an ovenproof dish. Add the meat and brown it all over. Pour on the wine and place the dish in a preheated moderate oven (180°C, 350°F, Gas Mark 4) to roast the meat. When the meat is about half cooked (about 25 minutes) add the peas, cover the dish with foil, and return it to the oven. Beat the eggs with the cheese, salt and parsley. When the meat is completely cooked (this takes about 45 minutes altogether) pour the egg mixture over it. Leave the dish in the oven long enough for the eggs to set, then remove from the oven and serve at once.

Serves 4

AGNELLO AL CARTOCCIO · PAPER-BAKED LAMB

In this speciality from the town of Modugno lamb chops are wrapped in paper and cooked with olives and *lampascioni* (or *lampasciuli*), those odd, bitter wild onions that are so popular throughout this region. I have never seen them outside southern Italy and have experimented by using ordinary onions instead. The result is good, though nowhere near as good as the original dish. If you happen to have this recipe with you on a self-catering holiday in Apulia you can of course buy the *lampascioni* locally. You will need 16 and they will have to be soaked in clean, cold water for 2 days before use.

> 8 lamb chops
> 16 small green olives
> 1 large onion, coarsely chopped
> salt and pepper
> olive oil

Place 2 chops each on the centre of four squares of oiled baking parchment. Put 4 olives on top of each pair of chops, cover with onion and season, then dribble a little oil on top. Wrap them up loosely and place on a baking tray in a preheated moderate oven (180°C, 350°F, Gas Mark 4) for 30 minutes. Serve wrapped up so each person can unwrap their own portion.

Serves 4

AGNELLO IN AGRODOLCE · SWEET AND SOUR LAMB

A distinctive Eastern influence can be tasted in all *agrodolce* recipes. Literally translated it means sweet and sour, though it bears little resemblance to Chinese food! It refers to a dish that is finished off with vinegar and sugar. Rabbit is also delicious cooked in this way.

1 large onion, thinly sliced
5 tablespoons olive oil
5 tablespoons milk
3 tablespoons tomato paste
1 kg/2 lb leg or shoulder of lamb, cubed
salt
1 wine glass best wine vinegar
pinch of black pepper
3 level tablespoons granulated sugar
4 fresh basil leaves

Fry the onion in the olive oil until golden. Mix the milk and tomato paste together. Add the lamb to the onion, brown all over and season with salt. Pour over the milk and tomato paste. Lower the heat, cover and cook slowly for about 40 minutes. Then pour in the vinegar, add the pepper and sugar, and cook for a further 15 minutes. Add the basil at the last minute and serve very hot.

Serves 6

AGNELLO ALLA CACCIATORA · HUNTER'S LAMB

This dish is wonderfully easy. The ingredients are all simply placed in a pot together and left in the oven for the flavours to blend. It is important to use the meat from leg of lamb for the best results.

800 g/1 lb 10 oz lamb steak (leg only), cubed
4 tablespoons olive oil
1 large onion, thickly sliced
400 g/13 oz potatoes, scrubbed and diced but unpeeled
500 g/1 lb ripe tomatoes, cut into quarters (or use
cherry tomatoes and leave them whole)
1 teaspoon dried oregano
salt and pepper

Arrange all the ingredients in a casserole dish and cover very tightly. Cook in the centre of a preheated warm oven (160°C, 325°F, Gas Mark 3) for 3 hours, stirring all the ingredients together occasionally, until the meat is tender.

Serves 4

BRASCIOLE ALLA BARESE · STUFFED STEAK ROLL

In Apulia, as in many parts of the south, stuffed meat olives like these are called *brasciole* or *braciole*. In other parts of the country this refers to chops. The original recipe calls for horse meat, which is very commonly used in the south. As it is rather unlikely that anyone in the UK would be able to get hold of horse meat even if they did want to use it, I have substituted beef, preferably well-seasoned and succulent beef that has been hung for at least three weeks.

> **4 slices rump steak, weighing 500 g/1 lb**
> **125 g/4 oz beef dripping**
> **125 g/4 oz Pecorino cheese**
> **salt and pepper**
> **fistful of fresh parsley**
> **4–8 cloves garlic**
> **4 tablespoons olive oil**
> **8 tablespoons passata (puréed tomatoes)**

Trim the meat and flatten it out with a meat hammer. If the slices are very large cut them in half. You should end up with neat rectangles of meat of even thickness. Arrange a strip of dripping and a strip of cheese down the centre of each slice of meat. Season. Lay parsley leaves over the cheese and dripping and put either a half or a whole clove of garlic on to each piece of meat. Roll them up and tie securely with thread. Heat the olive oil in a wide pan and add the passata. Season, cover and simmer for about 20 minutes. Put the *brasciole* into the tomato sauce and simmer very slowly for about 2 hours. Remove the thread before serving.

Serves 4

RAGÙ DEL MACELLAIO · BUTCHER'S OWN SAUCE

In typical Apulian style, this 'butcher's ragù' is made in such a way that the sauce cooked with the meat is used to dress pasta while the meat is served as a second course with vegetables and potatoes. One-pot cooking is very popular in Apulia. This recipe is a speciality of the city of Bari.

> **150–200 g/5–7 oz each of veal, pork, beef and lamb – any cut**
> **4 tablespoons olive oil**
> **1 large onion, thinly sliced**
> **400 g/13 oz ripe fresh tomatoes, peeled, deseeded and chopped, or use equivalent canned**
> **salt and pepper**

Cut all the meat into pieces no larger than a walnut. Heat the olive oil and fry the onion until golden. Add the meat and brown on all sides. Add the tomatoes and seasoning, cover and simmer for at least 1 hour. Dress orecchiette or cavatieddi with the sauce and serve the meat as a second course.

Serves 4

I DOLCI · DESSERTS, PIES AND PASTRIES

MARZAPANI BIANCHI DI GIOIA DEL COLLE · WHITE MARZIPAN CAKES

A very similar sweetmeat to these is *marzapane bianco di matino* as sold in and around Lecce. The only difference is that the latter tend to be less rich and are flavoured with cinnamon. In either case they are delicious and not difficult to make, perfect with cold white wine at the end of a meal for a really easy dessert.

> 500 g/1 lb blanched almonds
> 2 bitter almonds, blanched
> 500 g/1 lb granulated sugar
> 2 large eggs
> ½ teaspoon vanilla essence
> grated rind of 1 tangerine
> 2 level tablespoons plain white flour

Chop or process all the almonds to a fine, grainy powder, then mix with 450 g/14 oz of the sugar, the eggs, vanilla and tangerine rind. Knead with your fingers until you have a thick, doughy consistency. Break off pieces of the mixture and roll them into balls about the size of a walnut. Coat with the remaining sugar. Sprinkle the flour over a flat baking tray. Arrange the marzipan on it in neat rows and bake in a preheated moderate oven (180°C, 350°F, Gas Mark 4) for 20 minutes. Cool and serve.

Makes 20

RICOTTA DORATA · FRIED RICOTTA

Not to everyone's liking but worth trying is this delicious dessert of fried Ricotta. It really is exceptionally good if the Ricotta is fresh, and the fresher the better – perhaps best prepared on site by adventurous self-caterers. Ricotta is available all over Italy in varying degrees of quality. To make this a savoury dish, use the *piccante* (spicy and hot) version of the cheese and sprinkle with salt instead of sugar and cinnamon.

> **500 g/1 lb freshest possible Ricotta cheese**
> **olive oil for deep frying**
> **2 eggs, beaten**
> **6 level tablespoons plain white flour**
> **6 level tablespoons granulated sugar**

With a piece of thread, held at each end and pulled taut, slice the Ricotta very carefully and gently. Heat enough olive oil to fry all the cheese, preferably deep enough to fry both sides at once without turning them over. Dip the slices in the beaten egg, then in the flour. Fry each slice until golden and crisp, drain and keep warm until they are all fried. Sprinkle with the sugar and serve hot.

Serves 4

CIAMBELLA PUGLIESE · APULIAN RING CAKE

All over Italy *ciambella* is served at tea time as simple country fare, and is a delicious ring mould cake bursting with nourishment and flavour. The Apulian version is no exception, made with bread dough and potatoes for a really superb texture.

> **125 g/4 oz potatoes, peeled**
> **150 g/5 oz granulated sugar**

5 eggs
125 g/4 oz plain bread dough, fully risen (see basic
recipe, page 218)
50 g/2 oz lard
plain white flour
butter for greasing

Boil the potatoes until they are soft enough to mash. Mash while hot and mix with 125 g/4 oz of the sugar, the eggs, bread dough and lard. Knead very thoroughly, adding enough flour to make a smooth, elastic dough. Leave somewhere warm to rise for 24 hours or until doubled in size (in an Apulian summer you need only leave it overnight) then knead it again and form into a ring shape. Put into a thoroughly buttered and floured 28 cm/11 inch ring mould and leave to rise for about 1 hour in a warm spot. Bake in a preheated moderate oven (180°C, 350°F, Gas Mark 4) for approximately 1 hour. Cool, dust with the remaining sugar and serve.

Serves 8–10

CASSATA DI RICOTTA · RICOTTA CASSATA

This recipe is from the town of Modugno, though I'm told there are slight variations in other provinces. Completely different from the world-renowned Sicilian ice-cream concoction, this is a rich dessert – semi-pastry, semi-ice-cream – that never fails to impress but is surprisingly simple to make.

250 g/8 oz almonds (not blanched)
250 g/8 oz granulated sugar
4 tablespoons cold water
Madeira cake
150 ml/¼ pint white rum

325 g/11 oz fresh Ricotta cheese
50 g/2 oz assorted candied fruit, very finely chopped
pinch of cinnamon
grated rind of 1 lemon
50 g/2 oz cooking chocolate (Menier or Bournville),
broken into fragments (not grated)
approximately 125 g/4 oz almond paste (see below or
use ready made)

Take 5 almonds, toast in the oven and chop finely. Blanch the remaining almonds in boiling water for about 4 minutes, then peel and process to a fine powder. Set aside. Melt the sugar in a small pan over a low heat, add the water and stir to make a fairly runny caramel. Remove from heat. Cut circles out of the Madeira cake about 2.5 cm/1 inch thick, to fit the bottom of 16 7.5 cm/3 inch ramekins or similar-shaped moulds. Set aside.

Mix together the rum, Ricotta, chopped and the processed almonds, candied fruit, caramel, cinnamon, lemon rind, and finally the chocolate. Be very careful because it is important that the Ricotta stays completely white. If you stir too vigorously the chocolate will begin to melt and discolour the cheese. Fill the ramekins with this mixture, smoothing the top with care. Place in the fridge until hard – about 4 hours – then cover with a paper-thin sheet of almond paste (see below). Keep chilled until required.

Serves 16

ALMOND PASTE
125 g/4 oz blanched almonds
450 g/15 oz granulated sugar
1 wine glass cold water
30 g/1¼ oz glucose
icing sugar

Process the almonds to a fine powder. Sift and process again.

Repeat. Melt the sugar in a saucepan over a medium heat then add the cold water. Stir, then boil gently until a small amount pulled out with your index finger and your thumb and dipped in cold water will form a little ball when you rub it between your thumb and index finger. A less painful method is to pull the boiling sugar out with the point of a knife, *then* dip it in cold water, *then* rub it between your thumb and finger. When the caramel has passed this test, remove from the heat but do not allow to harden.

Process the powdered almonds and the glucose together. Then pour in the caramel and process to a smooth and even paste. Keep in a cool place (not the fridge) for half a day, or longer if necessary, then roll out very thinly, preferably on a marble slab, using icing sugar to prevent sticking as you would use flour with normal pastry.

LE CONSERVE · PRESERVES

CUPETA · ALMOND NOUGAT

I learned to make this delightful sweetmeat when I was given a colossal sack of almonds from a friend's tree and about halfway through was running out of ideas and the almonds were going bad! It's a kind of almond nougat sandwiched between rice paper and cut into whatever shape you like. They make great presents, being unusual and delicious.

500 g/1 lb almonds (not peeled or blanched)
500 g/1 lb granulated sugar

Process the almonds, but be careful; they should still be in small fragments rather than a fine powder or grains. Melt the sugar over a medium heat, then as soon as it starts to turn golden add the almonds. Stir with a wooden spoon; it should end up looking just like nougat. Wet a marble slab or table top with cold water and tip out the *cupeta*, smoothing it carefully with a wet spatula or knife until it is about 1 cm/½ inch thick. Let it cool down, but before it hardens completely, cut into strips about 2–3 cm/ ¾–1¼ inches wide and shape as you wish with your hands. Keep in a jar or tin for several months.

Makes about 500 g/1 lb

LATTE DI MANDORLE · ALMOND MILK

I had drunk the bought version of this almond milk many times in Italy, but to make it like this revealed a whole new range of possibilities for my tastebuds. If ever you are really overheated in southern Italy try this delicious local remedy.

500 g/1 lb ground almonds
cold water

Put the almonds in a bowl and cover with cold water, enough to come 5–6 cm/2–2½ inches over the nuts. Leave in a cool place to infuse for about 6 hours. Strain the liquid through muslin, squeezing the cloth to extract all the almond juice. Keep in a bottle in the fridge until required. This is a very thirst-quenching and refreshing drink, popular throughout the south.

Serves 4

THE WINES OF APULIA

The delicious, but extremely strong wines of Apulia were used almost solely as *vino da Taglio* until recently. This means that they were unlabelled wines with no DOC denomination, mixed with other wines from different parts of the country lacking in either flavour, strength or colour, to make up large quantities of *Vino da Tavola*, basic table wine as sold in supermarkets all over Italy. Throughout history, these wines have been famous for their potency but Apulia has only recently been able to produce its own DOC wines. At the 1985 trade fair – *Fiera del Levante* – twenty-one different DOC wines were presented, marking the start of a new era for Apulia's local resources. Only two per cent of Apulian wine is actually bottled and labelled! The rest is either sold *sfuso* (decanted from a barrel into unmarked containers) or becomes *vino da Taglio*. This means there is enormous potential in the future for the excellent wines of this region. However, do be warned, they are extremely strong! Undoubtedly it's not just the effects of the sun on the small, bushy vines scrambling across the ground that makes the wines so drinkable. There is also expertise, experience and a very efficient *ente regionale* – an organization that looks after the development of all the local agriculture.

Here are some of my personal favourites.

Aleatico A delicious sweet wine produced mainly in the province of Brindisi, where it is at its best, although the versions from Bari, Lecce and Taranto are also excellent. This extraordinary sweet red has a bouquet which makes it impossible to confuse it with any other wine. It is garnet coloured with a velvety smooth flavour and a superb sweetness. It should be served at room temperature as a dessert wine or as a drink in its own right.

Moscato As you get further south so the sweet wines come into their own. Here is Apulia's delicious Moscato, amber coloured, smooth and absolutely delicious. Very alcoholic and unique in character, it is best drunk as a dessert wine.

Ostuni A wine from Ostuni in the province of Brindisi which is available in both red and white. The white is very harmonious and dry, perfect for drinking with fish or with substantial antipasti. The red is more delicately flavoured with a gentle ruby colour and a slightly higher alcohol content. This is THE wine to drink with the famous soups of Apulia.

Primitivo di Manduria Rosso Used extensively as a *vino da Taglio* this is a naturally sweet wine, fruity and dry. It has a deep garnet colour and, aged at least six or seven years, is very similar to the best port wine.

Rosato del Salento As an incurable romantic I always fall for rosé wines, and this is a real find. It has a marvellous pale-pink colour and will stand up extremely well as a wine to drink throughout a meal – marries perfectly with cured meats and fish antipasti, cheeses, fried dishes, white meat and poultry.

Rosso di Barletta The most famous of Apulia's reds is this fine, full-bodied and very virile garnet-coloured wine made from an amazing collection of different vines: *Uva di Troija*, *Negro Amaro*, *Ciliegiolo*, *Montepulciano*, *Barbera* and *Sangiovese*. This is a wine that deserves to be looked after with great care, preferably put away in a cool cellar.

San Severo This is the best known of all the white wines of Apulia and lends itself to an amazing number of gastronomic marriages, especially those based on seafood. It is a really fine, elegant white wine with a pale, straw-yellow colour and a neutral, dry flavour – fairly alcoholic at approximately 14 degrees, so beware!

Rosé and red versions are also produced, though they tend to be less well known. The red starts out ruby coloured but develops a lovely brick colour as it ages. It is generally served with light roasts or stews. The rosé is a perfect antipasto wine.

· BASILICATA ·

To many Italians this very dry, arid, bitter region with its stony, brown soil and rocky, ugly hills is still known as Lucania. The Lucani were the original inhabitants, and when Caesar Augustus made it into the official third region of Italy by uniting it with Calabria, then called Bruttium, Lucania was the name of the region. The Byzantines then renamed it from the word *basilikos*, meaning governor or prince. In the twelfth century, under the Normans, it continued to be called Basilicata, and it was not until 1932 that the name reverted to the original Lucania. In 1947 a final compromise was reached: the region is officially named Basilicata, but its inhabitants are called Lucani.

The landscape is almost completely hilly or mountainous, broken up by wide valleys that drop downwards to the rivers flowing through to the narrow coastal plain. Once this was a green, densely wooded and beautiful region but now it is desolate, arid land, eroded by nature and humanity. It is rare to see isolated houses, yet the tiny villages and small towns are situated very far apart, often at the feet of an ancient ruined castle on the brow of a craggy hill. The region has two tiny strips of coastline – to the east the Adriatic, and to the west the Thyrrhenian – but there are no important ports here, just as there are no true urban centres. In the extreme north the ashes of the dead volcano – Monte Vulture – have granted the soil some fertility. This means that in the lower valleys there are olive groves and vineyards, while higher up are patches of dense woodland – beeches, chestnut trees and oaks – that remind one of what it was once like here until it was deforested by foreign invaders and the Romans. (The British shipbuilding industry used to use wood from here.) The sloping hills that lead down to the gulf of Taranto are sparse and bare, with a few juniper bushes and other scrubby bushes growing out of the stony ground, and the odd pine tree standing awkwardly among the desolation as a reminder of the old days.

The two coastlines are totally different from each other. On the Ionian, the coast is low and smooth, whereas on the Tyrrhenian it is broken up by cliffs, rocky promontories and pretty bays, all enlivened by quite thick, lush vegetation. The narrow plain lying inside the coastline on the Ionian, is twenty by thirty kilometres. It represents less than ten per cent of the entire region, and it is where most of the crop growing and stock raising takes place. Until recently it was malaria-ridden, filthy bog; now it is reclaimed and drained soil, but there is so little of it.

The region does have waterways, but they are mostly unruly torrents that alternate between long periods of total dryness and flooding. Without the woodland that the region desperately needs, the torrential nature of the waterways is accentuated, and as they flood they tear away at the soil's humus, leaving nothing behind but sand and stones. The inland areas suffer from harsh winters with winds blowing from the south-east. On the coast, this means mild winters but scorching hot summers.

Basilicata is one of the least populated regions in the entire country, a region which for centuries has suffered from isolation and abandonment. Poverty has always forced the Lucani to emigrate, and according to popular opinion there are more Lucani spread around the globe than there are living in the region itself.

There are just two provinces in this region. Potenza is the capital of the first province and sits 800 metres above sea level, making it one of the highest cities in Italy. Potenza has developed quickly in the last few decades, though it is still principally an agricultural centre with a few industries and factories dotted around its outskirts. It is a completely mountainous province, crossed by rivers and streams. To the north in the Vulture area is the agricultural centre of Melfi, which used to be the residence of the Norman kings in the eleventh and twelfth centuries. All around this relatively fertile zone there are several small industries such as olive oil presses, pasta factories and wine centres. Avigliano is the local craftwork centre and is also famous for its wine; Lauria is a sheep-farming centre. Not far away, tucked in between the mountains and looking across the lovely Golfo di Policastro, is Maratea, which dominates one of the most stunning of Italy's bays and where the resort of Marina di Maratea is situated. The earthquake in 1980, which affected parts of Basilicata and Campania, has completely destroyed many of the villages in this province.

Matera, the capital city of Basilicata's other province, is a unique and extraordinary city. It has two separate faces, the old and the new, and as so often is the case, it is the old which is so remarkable. Matera has long been known as the city of stones, but the stones are now just historical monuments, recalling times of despair. In the sides of an enormous rocky ravine around a cone-shaped hill, there are thousands of caves and niches, connected to each other by tiny alleys and steep steps hewn from the rock. They cannot be called rooms, as they are really no more than shelters from the outside elements, but since the earliest recorded history of the area, this soft rock has been chiselled and hacked into shape to create 'homes' for thousands of families. In this horrendous, damp, filthy, human anthill there lived until very recently a whole race of modern-day cave people. Nowadays the stones are almost completely uninhabited, and the people have been transferred into specially built new suburbs where they can be housed in a manner befitting civilized human beings. The modern city has sprung up in the last thirty-five years and is filled with tall apartment blocks and tree-lined avenues. This is an agricultural centre with a few minor industries. The hilly province continues down to the coastal plain, where Lido di Metaponto is the only seaside resort in the province. Along this brief stretch of coast are the ruined remains of many Greek colonies that once prospered here. Metaponto was one of these, as was Eraclea, which is nowadays the main agricultural centre in the reclaimed marsh.

Traditionally the inhabitants of this region work the land, even though there is very little fertile ground. The climate tends to be unhelpful, irrigation is almost impossible due to the nature of the soil, and there is a tendency to favour the most antiquated and outdated farming methods such as mule-drawn ploughs. Mostly, the region produces grain wheat, barley and oats, and also sugar beet, olives and vines. To a lesser degree but on the increase, nectarines, peaches, tomatoes, strawberries, figs, walnuts and almonds thrive well.

In the mountain pastures and grazing areas, sheep farming predominates, yielding good-quality wool and cheese. Pigs and cows are also bred in the reclaimed areas. Industry is still very scarce, mostly given over to the development of locally produced goods such as oil, wine, cheese, wool, pasta, sugar and flour. Methane has been recently discovered here and has made some impact, with factories now using it to produce plastic goods and chemicals. Cottage industries such as pottery, iron and ceramics satisfy some of the local people's immediate needs and are scattered all over the region. Tourism simply does not figure in the region's economy, and there are only a few places of interest for the visitor who ventures down here: the lakes of Monticchio situated in the volcanic craters of Monte Vulture, which have natural spring water flowing from them; Policore with its ancient ruins; and the beaches of Maratea and Metaponte. Matera is the only city in Italy not connected to the national railway system, and the motorway only briefly touches the region along the Tyrrhenian coast, so communication with the rest of Italy remains antiquated and difficult – not the best way to attract tourists. New roads are being built towards the centre of the region, following the valleys of the four major rivers, and it is to be hoped this will mean the beginning of the end of Basilicata's isolation.

The region's main problems are lack of irrigation and reforestation. The region is rich in water but it must be tamed and disciplined, like the dams on the Bradane and Afri. These dams have permitted large areas to be irrigated and turned into green orchards and fields. The secular poverty of this place has led its inhabitants to destroy the woodland in order to make space for pasture land or grain fields, but in this way the natural balance of the soil has been destroyed. Landslides and earthquakes are a fact of life in Basilicata and the damage they cause is enormous. Reforestation is a desperate need, but progress is painfully slow. Overshadowing all other considerations is the process of recovering from the 1980 earthquake. The fact that the region was used as a dumping ground for Jews and 'undesirables' during the Fascist regime makes it seem even more unappealing, and it is largely ignored by the rest of the country. Yet if you look, there is beauty here, a desolate, rugged, unspoilt loveliness that makes it impossible to forget.

What memories will the visitor take away, apart from images of endless, desertlike scenery, of steep rocks, olive groves, prickly pear groves, and fields of wild tomatoes? What will you remember, apart from the gentle hospitality of these humble people of few words? Their cuisine is unforgettable; butter is hardly ever used, and who needs it when the olive oil has such a deep intense flavour and texture? The strong, heady wines are equally memorable, bursting with the heat of the sun. But you'll also remember black-shrouded women bent over their tables, endlessly making their own particular type of pasta, rolling, twisting and shaping it with age-old expertise before tossing it into a pot of boiling water to cook, then dressing it with fiery, red sauces vigorously flavoured with chilli, herbs and the unique wild tomato, and all finished off with clouds of pungent Pecorino cheese.

Pasta rules here: pasta cooked in a hundred different hand-made shapes and forms, to fill hungry bellies and ward off misery and sadness; pasta dressed in red, green or yellow is the basis of everything, because meat hardly features in this cuisine. What meat there is is generally mutton, lamb or kid, and therefore soup is very rare too – how can you make a proper soup without meat or chicken stock? Not only is there no proper first course in the form of a soup, there is also no main meat and vegetable course. Pasta, the very special, local-cured meats, vegetables, and cheese make up the local range of goods. The prosciutto and salami of Basilicata are fine and lean, often prepared in olive oil to keep them moist and fragrant. The most fragrant of all its sausages is the *luganega*, the long continuous coil of sausage copied all over the world and used a great deal in all manner of dishes. Vegetables are often cooked in a stew or casserole so as to make them substantial enough for a main course dish, served in vast portions.

Just because meat and fish are not readily available here does not mean the Lucani have simply stopped bothering to cook; this is a region where the imagination has been put to excellent use and has made the best of what there is. There are delicious fish dishes from the lovely seaside resort of Maratea and superb lamb dishes from the shepherd traditions of the hills. And the cheeses are remarkable. What rich northern industrialist does not enjoy at least one or two of these excellent local cheeses that have been made to perfection for so many centuries? The smooth Mozzarella, the excellent Provolone, the delicious Caciocavallo – all these and many more are produced here, and eaten all over Italy.

Wonderful old Lucania, where Horace himself brought his cook to learn how to prepare these ancient, delightfully simple and very healthy dishes. Much loved and maligned Basilicata, where history and nature have never been kind, but where the sting of chilli pepper and the scent of herbs rises above all adversity.

ANTIPASTI · ANTIPASTI

CIPOLLE FRITTE CON I CAPPERI · FRIED ONIONS WITH CAPERS

I came across this rather weird antipasto in a restaurant in Matera, where antipasti seem to feature very strongly in the presentation of a meal. In a region where there is virtually no meat and, once away from the seashore, very little fish, strong, satisfying flavours come into their own. I find there is a slight feeling of anticlimax in a meal where there are a lot of antipasti but little or nothing to follow the mood. However, here is the recipe for this very powerful dish, served with PLENTY of bread.

> **2 large white onions, thinly sliced**
> **3 tablespoons olive oil, butter or cooking oil**
> **4 tablespoons small capers, rinsed and lightly dried**
> **2 tablespoons dried red chilli peppers, finely chopped**

Fry the onions in the fat until soft and just coloured. Mix in the capers, then arrange in a dish, scatter the chilli over and serve. You may chill this dish until required if you wish.

Serves 4

BRUSCHETTA ALL'OLIO SANTO · BRUSCHETTA WITH HOLY OIL

The first time I took a bite of this seemingly innocent-looking slice of toast I thought I was quite literally going to catch fire. The local condiment of Holy Oil is nothing more than virgin olive oil into which fiery red chilli peppers (lots and lots of them!) are crushed and left to blacken and disintegrate. In Basilicata, and indeed all over the south once you get past Foggia, *olio santo* will appear on the table so that you can pour it on to your food like ketchup or mustard! Apparently it is a legacy of the time when diseases such as malaria and cholera were part of daily life in the region. Prepared like this, the three elements which best typify this cuisine appear as one: olive oil, chillis and bread.

1 large slice coarse Italian bread with crusts
1 large clove garlic, peeled
3 tablespoons olive oil
1 large red chilli pepper, chopped and crushed
salt

Toast the bread on both sides until crisp and golden. Rub it thoroughly with the garlic on both sides and put it on a plate. Mix the oil and crushed chilli together very thoroughly (this can be done the day before for a really eye-watering effect) then pour it over the toast, sprinkle with salt and serve.

Serves 1

LE MINESTRE · SOUP

MINESTRA STRASCINATA · RAGGED SOUP

Soup doesn't really feature in the Lucanian cuisine. With very little meat cookery going on, except for lamb in spring and a little pork in autumn, there is no basis for the creation of soups because the bones and carcasses with which to make the broth or stock essential to proper soup are virtually non-existent. This is the nearest thing to a soup I could find. As far as antipasti go, you are most likely to be served a dish containing a selection of the delicious local salumi such as salame, prosciutto, sausages and so on – all extremely moist, soft and lean, perfect with crusty bread, plenty of heartwarming wine and a handful of olives.

Ideally you should use the traditional implement to cut the pasta for this soup, but as it is very difficult to use and equally hard to obtain anywhere outside the region I have adapted the recipe slightly.

> **400 g/13 oz strong white flour**
> **1 heaped tablespoon lard**
> **1 onion, finely chopped**
> **2 cloves garlic, chopped**
> **2 tablespoons olive oil**
> **500 g/1 lb canned tomatoes, chopped**
> **salt and pepper**
> **200 g/7 oz Pecorino cheese, grated**

Put the flour on the table in a hill shape and make a hole in the centre with your fist. Put a pinch of salt and the lard into the hole, then knead together to make a stiff dough, adding as much water as you need. Work this dough for about 30 minutes, then roll it out as thinly as possible. Using a very sharp knife, cut the dough into small uneven pieces about 1 cm/½ inch square.

Fry the onion and garlic with the olive oil, then when the onion is translucent add the tomatoes and seasoning. Stir together, and cook over a low heat for about 20 minutes. Bring a large pot of salted water to the boil, toss in the pasta squares and boil for about 5 minutes. Drain the pasta, but leave it fairly wet, transfer to a warm bowl and pour over the sauce and the cheese. Toss it all together and serve. This kind of pasta has the advantage of never overcooking even if it's left to sit for a while.

Serves 4

PASTA · PASTA

PASTA CON RAGÙ ALLA POTENTINA · PASTA WITH POTENZA SAUCE

Poverty is still fairly widespread in the south, so one-pot cooking is very common. *Ragù alla potentina* is a meat and tomato sauce for pasta with the meat taken out and served as a second course. The sauce suits all kinds of pasta but traditionally you should serve it with a classic, homemade local version.

> 50 g/2 oz fresh parsley
> 1 large clove garlic, peeled
> pinch of red chilli powder
> pinch of freshly grated nutmeg
> 50 g/2 oz Pecorino cheese
> 1 slice of pork or beef, weighing approximately
> 625 g/1 lb 4 oz, beaten flat and thin
> 75 g/3 oz streaky bacon or pancetta, thickly sliced
> 50 g/2 oz lard
> 3 tablespoons olive oil
> 1 glass dry white wine
> 500 g/1 lb canned or fresh tomatoes, peeled, deseeded
> and coarsely chopped
> salt and pepper
> 625 g/1 lb 4 oz any chunky pasta

Chop the parsley with the garlic, put in a bowl and mix in the chilli and nutmeg. Chop half the cheese, grate the rest, then add it all to the parsley and garlic mixture. Spread this on to the meat and lay the bacon on the top. Roll up the meat and tie securely with thread to prevent it coming apart during cooking.

Fry the lard and oil together in a pan until sizzling hot, then lay the meat in it and brown all over. Add a little wine every now and again for extra moisture and when the meat roll is sealed all over, lower the heat and add the tomatoes. Season, cover and simmer for at least 2 hours, adding a little water occasionally to prevent it drying out.

Bring a large pot of salted water to the boil and toss in the pasta. Meanwhile take the meat roll out of the pot and push the sauce through a sieve. Drain the pasta and transfer it to a warm bowl, pour over the sauce and toss thoroughly before serving. Serve the meat roll separately as a second course.

Serves 6

MACCHERONI DI FUOCO · MACARONI ON FIRE

There is no better way to keep hunger at bay than to murder it with chilli! A very old local recipe, this is a dish of pasta that sets your insides on fire – the first time I had it I was innocently under the impression that the redness belonged to tomato sauce . . . Please warn your family and friends!

> **400 g/13 oz bucatini or other chunky pasta**
> **1 wine glass olive oil**
> **4 cloves garlic, peeled**
> **4 whole red chilli peppers**

Put a large pot of salted water on to boil for the pasta. Meanwhile heat half the oil in a cast-iron frying pan until it sizzles. Add 3 cloves of garlic then add the chillis, and as soon as they have swollen up and become shiny, remove both the garlic and the chillis from the pan. Process or pound them together to form a smooth paste.

Toss the pasta into the boiling water and cook until *al dente*. Pour the remaining oil into the cast-iron pan, add the remaining clove of garlic and fry until golden. Remove the garlic from the oil and stir in the prepared chilli paste, mixing it all up together to make a smooth sauce. Be careful not to let the sauce blacken – it can start to happen very quickly.

Drain the pasta and transfer to a warmed bowl. Pour over the sauce and toss it all together. Serve this lovely, bright-red dish at once.

Serves 4

LAGANE E FAGIOLI · PASTA RIBBONS WITH BEANS

One of the oldest pasta dishes in the entire country, a simple and obviously poor combination of food: pasta and beans in its plainest form. It is best to use fresh borlotti or cannellini beans but if these are difficult to obtain, use the dried version of either.

> 500 g/1 lb cannellini or borlotti beans, fresh or dried
> 625 g/1 lb 4 oz strong white flour
> 2 tablespoons olive oil
> 2 cloves garlic, peeled and lightly crushed
> large pinch of red chilli powder
> salt

If using dried beans, soak overnight in cold water. The next day, bring to a fast boil in fresh water then drain. At this point they can be used exactly like the fresh version.

Cook the beans in plenty of water over a low heat so that they boil steadily but gently. Put the flour on the table top and make a hole in the centre with your fist. Pour in enough water to make a smooth, elastic dough. Knead for a few minutes, then roll out and cut into wide, irregular strips – these are the lagane. When you are just about ready to eat, boil the pasta in plenty of salted water for 3–4 minutes (test one before you decide they're done; cooking times vary so much for homemade pasta) with a little olive oil to prevent sticking. (As this is a very big pasta you will need a very big pot and lots of water.) Heat the olive oil in a small pan with the garlic and chilli. Drain the beans and pasta and transfer to a warm bowl. Pour over the hot oil with the garlic and chilli and toss them all together. Season with salt and remove the cloves of crushed garlic just before serving.

Serves 6

RAVIOLI CON LA RICOTTA · RAVIOLI WITH RICOTTA

I like these ravioli because they are so easy to make! They are delicious no matter what sauce you use to dress them.

> **500 g/1 lb strong white flour**
> **6 eggs**
> **salt**
> **250 g/8 oz fresh Ricotta or other creamy fresh cheese**
> **50 g/2 oz fresh parsley, chopped**
> **9 tablespoons grated Pecorino cheese**
> **ragù alla Potentina (see recipe page 114)**
> **1 teaspoon chilli powder**

Put the flour on the table and make a hole in the centre with your fist. Break 3 of the eggs into the hole and add a pinch of salt. Knead carefully until smooth and elastic, then cover with a cloth and leave to rest for about 30 minutes.

Mash the Ricotta with the parsley, 4 tablespoons of the Pecorino and the remaining eggs to make a filling for the ravioli. Set it aside. Roll out the dough to a thin sheet and cut into 7.5 cm/3 inch circles using a glass or a round pastry cutter. Put a teaspoonful of the filling in the centre of each circle and cover with a second circle, sealing the edges together very carefully so none of the filling escapes during the cooking. Put a large pot of salted water on to boil and as soon as it is boiling fast, toss the ravioli in one at a time. Scoop them out with a slotted spoon as soon as they are cooked – about 6–8 minutes. Turn into a warmed bowl and dress with the hot ragù. Scatter the remaining Pecorino and the chilli powder over the top and mix together with great care before serving.

Serves 4

STRANGULAPREUTI · PRIEST STRANGLERS

This is the local version of savoury 'priest stranglers'; they also appear in other areas, but in the deep south there is a very strong feeling about religion, as there has been for several centuries. There are two theories about the origins of the name. The first is that as priests were traditionally greedy and gluttonous, their favourite dish would be prepared for them when they came to visit in the hope that they'd choke on it! The second is that the dish had some quality about it which would successfully strangle a priest and stop him preaching! There has long been a strong pagan influence on the local beliefs – not all of which concur with those of the Catholic church!

> **625 g/1 lb 4 oz strong white flour**
> **ragù alla Potentina (see recipe page 114)**
> **5 tablespoons grated Pecorino cheese**
> **large pinch of chilli powder**
> **salt**

Put all the flour except 2 tablespoons on the table and make a hole in the centre with your fist. Pour a few tablespoons of boiling water into the centre (start with 4 and add more if required) and mix fast and furiously with a wooden spoon. As soon as the mixture has amalgamated, use your hands to knead together for

15 minutes to a smooth and elastic dough. Roll out into snakes about the thickness of a finger and cut into 2 cm/¾ inch lengths. Using the remaining flour to prevent sticking, squash the pieces of dough downwards against the table top to make them concave. Heat the sauce and bring a large pot of salted water to the boil. Toss in the 'priest stranglers'. They will all immediately float on the surface of the water and should descend to the bottom of the pot when they are cooked. At this point, drain and transfer to a warm bowl, pour over the hot ragù and toss. Scatter on the cheese and chilli powder, toss once again and serve.

Serves 4

I LEGUMI · VEGETABLES

PATATE AL FORNO RAGANATE · BAKED POTATOES WITH CHEESE AND BREADCRUMBS

It is with the vegetable dishes that the local cooks are really inspired. There are countless combinations of vegetable dishes that really make up for the absence of a proper main dish – meat or fish are saved for special occasions. In this recipe potatoes are layered with oregano, tomatoes and onions then baked in the oven.

800 g/1 lb 10 oz old potatoes
500 g/1 lb onions
500 g/1 lb tomatoes
large wine glass of olive oil
dried oregano
5 tablespoons grated Pecorino cheese
5 tablespoons dried breadcrumbs
salt

Peel and slice the potatoes and onions to roughly the same size, then peel and slice the tomatoes. Use a little of the oil to grease an ovenproof dish and layer the vegetables with a few drops of olive oil, a pinch of oregano, a spoonful each of cheese and breadcrumbs and a little salt in between each layer. Bake in a preheated warm oven (160°C, 325°F, Gas Mark 3) for about 1 hour before serving.

Serves 4

CAPPELLE DI FUNGHI AL FORNO · BAKED MUSHROOMS

A wonderfully simple recipe for getting the best flavour out of mushrooms. You should use porcini (*Boletus edulis*) for this dish, but if these are unavailable, use the largest and tastiest mushrooms you can find.

> **8 large mushrooms, stalks removed**
> **fistful of fresh parsley**
> **2 cloves garlic, peeled**
> **2 tablespoons breadcrumbs**
> **1 wine glass olive oil**
> **salt**
> **chilli powder**
> **dried oregano**

Clean the mushrooms and brush them carefully to remove any grit. Chop the parsley with the garlic then mix with the breadcrumbs and about a third of the oil. Season to taste with salt and chilli powder. Oil an ovenproof dish and lay the mushrooms in it facing upwards. Cover with the parsley mixture and then sprinkle with oregano and the remaining oil. Bake in a preheated warm oven (160°C, 325°F, Gas Mark 3) for 10 minutes before serving. Excellent with grilled meat.

Serves 4

CALZONE DI VERDURA · ENDIVE (OR SWISS CHARD) PASTY

fistful of black olives or sultanas
1 kg/2 lb endive or Swiss chard
salt
1 dried chilli pepper, crumbled up
approximately 6 tablespoons olive oil
300 g/10 oz strong white flour
50 g/2 oz prepared bread dough, fully risen (see basic recipe page 218)

If using olives stone them; if using sultanas, cover them with warm water and leave to soak for 15 minutes. Wash and trim the endive or chard, removing all hard stalks. Cut into strips and put in a bowl with the olives or sultanas, a pinch of salt, the chilli pepper, and about 4 tablespoons olive oil. Mix together and set aside. Put the flour on the table, add a pinch of salt, 2 tablespoons of the oil and the bread dough. Knead together to make a smooth dough, then roll out and lay half (without cutting it) on an oiled baking tray. Cover this half with the prepared endive or chard and flap the other half over it. Pinch the edges securely closed, brush with more oil and bake in a preheated moderate oven (180°C, 350°F, Gas Mark 4) for 30 minutes. This can be served cold but is best hot.

Serves 4–6

CIAMMOTTA · VEGETABLE STEW

Famous all over Italy and thought by many to be among ratatouille's ancestors, this is a really superb vegetable stew. I prefer it cold.

250 g/8 oz aubergines
250 g/8 oz potatoes
200 g/7 oz tomatoes
250 g/8 oz peppers
6 tablespoons olive oil
1 clove garlic, crushed
salt and pepper

Slice the aubergines, lay them in a colander and sprinkle with plenty of salt. Cover with a plate, put a weight on top and leave in the sink for the bitter juices to drain out while you prepare the rest of the vegetables. Peel and dice the potatoes, peel, deseed and chop the tomatoes, and deseed and slice the peppers. Heat half the olive oil, wash and dry the aubergines and fry in the oil until crisp on the outside. In a separate pan fry the peppers and potatoes together in the remaining oil until just soft. Then add the aubergines, tomatoes and garlic, season and simmer for 1 hour. Serve hot or cold.

Serves 4

MELANZANE AL FORNO · BAKED AUBERGINES

This is the original stuffed aubergine dish! All the ingredients so much favoured by local cooks are here: capers, olives, garlic, anchovies and tomatoes.

1 kg/2 lb oval-shaped aubergines
salt
1 stale white bread roll
150 g/5 oz black olives, stoned (and chopped if they
are very large)
fistful of fresh parsley, chopped
1 clove garlic, chopped

125 g/4 oz canned or salted anchovies
50 g/2 oz capers, chopped
large pinch of dried oregano
2 very ripe tomatoes, cut into strips
½ wine glass olive oil

Cut the aubergines in half lengthways and slice into the flesh on the diagonal about 1 cm/½ inch deep, all over both surfaces of each half. Sprinkle with salt and leave upside down in a colander over the sink so all the bitter juices can seep out. Meanwhile, break open the roll and remove the soft bread from inside the crust. Crumble it up into a bowl and add the olives, parsley and garlic. Wash and chop the anchovies, removing any bones, and add with the capers and oregano to the bread mixture. Wash and pat dry the aubergines and put them in an oiled ovenproof dish, facing upwards. Scatter the bread mixture all over and cover with strips of tomato. Dribble the olive oil all over the top and bake in a preheated warm oven (160°C, 325°F, Gas Mark 3) for about 1 hour. Serve warm.

Serves 4

I PESCI · FISH

SCAPICE · MARINATED ANCHOVIES

One of the fish specialities of this region is this strange and very Eastern dish of marinated fried anchovies. Any other small and oily fish works just as well.

1 kg/2 lb fresh anchovies or similar small fish, gutted, scaled and heads removed

oil for deep frying
2 level tablespoons plain white flour
200 ml/7 fl oz wine vinegar
2 cloves garlic, peeled and lightly crushed
fistful of fresh mint leaves
2 red chilli peppers

Wash the fish then set them aside to dry out. Heat the oil for frying. Toss the dry fish in the flour to cover them lightly, then cook in the hot oil. When they are crisp and golden scoop them out with a slotted spoon and drain on kitchen paper. Heat the vinegar with the garlic, mint and whole chillis until boiling, then pour over the fried fish. Cover and leave to marinate for about a day before serving as an antipasto or part of a fish course. It will keep in a cool place for up to 6 days.

Serves 4–6

BACCALÀ ALLA POTENTINA · SALT COD CASSEROLE WITH OLIVES

800 g/1 lb 10 oz dried salt cod (stockfish), soaked overnight
50 g/2 oz sultanas
½ wine glass olive oil
1 large onion, finely sliced
1 tablespoon tomato paste
125 g/4 oz black olives, stoned

Cut up the fish, removing any bones, then wash and dry it. Cover the sultanas with warm water and leave to soak. Heat the olive oil in a pan and add the onion. Fry until golden then add the fish. Dilute the tomato paste in a little water, and add to the pan, then stir in the olives and the drained sultanas. Cover and simmer on a very low heat for about 1 hour, adding a little water to prevent drying out. The *baccala* is traditionally served with fried red and yellow peppers.

Serves 4

BACCALÀ ALLA LUCANA · SALT COD WITH PICKLED PEPPERS

This is the classic dish of wintertime, using stockfish and pre-served peppers when there are almost no fresh goods available – but the end result is excellent.

> **800 g/1 lb 10 oz dried salt cod (stockfish) soaked overnight**
> **½ wine glass olive oil**
> **8–10 peppers preserved in vinegar (*peperoni sott'aceto*)**

Cut the fish into strips, remove any bones, then wash and dry. Heat the oil in a pan with the peppers then add the fish and brown on all sides. Lower the heat and simmer for 30 minutes. Serve hot or cold.

Serves 4

ZUPPA DI PESCE · FISH SOUP

> **1 kg/2 lb cleaned fish – dentex, mullet, bass or other; a wide mixture is preferable**
> **2 cloves garlic, lightly crushed**
> **½ wine glass olive oil**

50 g/2 oz fresh parsley, chopped
½ teaspoon red chilli powder
4 slices coarse white bread with thick crusts

Prepare the fish and cut into large chunks. Fry the garlic in the oil until brown, then scoop it out and discard. Add the fish to the pan, brown it all over, then scatter the parsley over the top. Sprinkle with the chilli powder, then cover and simmer for 30 minutes. Toast the bread in the oven and place one slice each on four plates, pour the 'soup' over the bread and serve.

Serves 4

TORTIERA DI BACCALÀ E PATATE · SALT COD PIE WITH POTATOES

800 g/1 lb 10 oz old potatoes
625 g/1 lb 4 oz dried salt cod (stockfish), soaked
overnight then washed and dried
1 glass olive oil
3 tablespoons fresh or dried white breadcrumbs
dried oregano
3 large cloves garlic, peeled and chopped
red chilli pepper, chopped
salt
juice of ½ lemon

Peel the potatoes and boil until just tender. Boil the fish until tender. Drain both. Slice the potatoes, then clean and de-bone the fish before cutting it into pieces the same size as the potato slices. Use a little of the oil to grease an ovenproof dish or baking tray and scatter half the breadcrumbs over the bottom. Arrange a layer of potatoes in the dish, then add a layer of fish. Dress each layer with a few drops of oil, a pinch of oregano, a few pieces of garlic and chilli, and a very small pinch of salt. When all the ingredients are used up, cover the top with the remaining breadcrumbs and oil. Bake in a preheated moderate oven (180°C, 350°F, Gas Mark 4) for 40 minutes and sprinkle with the lemon juice before serving.

Serves 4

LE CARNI · MEAT

PIGNATA DI PECORA · MUTTON CASSEROLE

The secret of success for this delicious and simple mutton stew is to use a tight-fitting lid on the pot.

> 1 kg/2 lb mutton (leg or shoulder), diced
> 300 g/10 oz potatoes, peeled and diced
> 300 g/10 oz onions, finely chopped
> 1 large celery stick, finely chopped
> 200 g/7 oz ripe tomatoes, peeled, deseeded and coarsely chopped
> 125 g/4 oz coarse sausage or salame, finely chopped
> 1 large pinch red chilli powder
> salt
> 250 ml/8 fl oz cold water
> 200 g/7 oz Pecorino cheese, grated

Put the mutton, potatoes, onions, celery and tomatoes into a casserole; scatter the chopped sausage, sprinkle on the chilli powder, season with salt and pour over the water. Cover with a tight-fitting lid and simmer over a very low heat for 1½ hours or until the meat is tender. Serve the grated Pecorino cheese separately.

Serves 6

AGNELLO E FUNGHI AL FORNO · ROAST LAMB WITH MUSHROOMS

An unusual but excellent combination for a casserole is lamb with mushrooms, preferably wild ones.

> **625 g/1 lb 4 oz wild mushrooms**
> **1 kg/2 lb lamb leg steaks**
> **pinch of red chilli pepper**
> **salt**
> **4 tablespoons olive oil**

Clean the mushrooms and set aside. Trim and cube the lamb steaks then put into a saucepan. Scatter the mushrooms over the meat, season with the chilli and salt and pour the oil over the top. Cover and simmer for about 1¼ hours, basting occasionally with the juices from the mushrooms. Serve immediately.

Serves 4

CUTURIDDI · LAMB AND TOMATO CASSEROLE

> **1 kg/2 lb shoulder and breast of lamb, trimmed and cubed**
> **1 large stick celery, cut into large sections**
> **6–7 button onions, peeled**
> **2 large tomatoes, peeled, deseeded and chopped**

1 sprig fresh rosemary
2 bay leaves
salt
pinch of chilli powder

Put the meat in a large saucepan. Scatter the celery and onions over, then add the tomatoes, rosemary and bay leaves. Add just enough water to cover the meat, season with salt and chilli, then cover and simmer for 1½ hours. Taste and adjust seasoning before serving.

Serves 4

I POLLI · POULTRY AND GAME

POLLO ALLA POTENTINA · CHICKEN CASSEROLE WITH HERBS

A very rare appearance by the humble chicken in the kitchens of Basilicata, where it is casseroled with herbs, tomatoes, wine, onion and the inevitable chilli.

30 g/1¼ oz lard
4 tablespoons olive oil
1 chicken, weighing approximately 1.2 kg/2 lb 7 oz, jointed
1 large onion, sliced
1 large glass dry white wine
large pinch of red chilli powder
fistful of fresh parsley, chopped
fistful of fresh basil, chopped

300 g/10 oz ripe tomatoes, peeled, deseeded and chopped
salt

Heat the lard and oil together in a casserole, add the chicken joints and brown them all over. Add the onion and continue to cook, turning the chicken over occasionally and wetting it with the wine a little at a time. Sprinkle with the chilli. When all the wine has been absorbed or has evaporated, add the herbs and tomatoes, season with salt, cover and leave to simmer for about 1 hour, adding a little water if necessary to prevent it drying out. Serve hot, accompanied by roast potatoes and mushrooms.

Serves 4

BECCACCE IN SALMÌ · BRAISED WOODCOCK

A very unusual way of serving woodcock. Other game birds, such as pigeon, can also be prepared in this way.

2 woodcocks, well hung then plucked and thoroughly gutted
salt
125 g/4 oz prosciutto crudo (Parma ham)
2 tablespoons olive oil
½ glass dry white wine
½ glass Marsala
2 tablespoons cooking oil
1 tablespoon capers (preferably salted), washed and chopped
2 salted or canned anchovies, washed and chopped
giblets from the birds, trimmed, washed and finely chopped
8 slices white Italian bread

Prepare the woodcocks and salt them carefully, inside and out. Wrap them up in the ham, then heat the oil in a deep pan and lay the birds in it. Brown them all over, sprinkling with some of the wine and Marsala, then cover and leave to simmer gently. Heat the cooking oil in a separate pan, add the capers and anchovies and fry gently to a creamy texture. Add the giblets, stir together and simmer. Pour the remaining wine and Marsala into the pan containing the woodcocks and cook for a further 30 minutes. Toast the bread and spread the hot giblet mixture on to it. Place the woodcocks in the centre of a serving platter and surround with the juices from the pot. Put the prepared toast around the edges and serve immediately.

Serves 4

I DOLCI · PIES, PASTRIES AND DESSERTS

CUCCIA · WHEAT GRAIN AND CHOCOLATE PUDDING

> 125 g/4 oz wheat grains
> 4 tablespoons sugar
> 50 g/2 oz bitter chocolate, chopped
> ½ pomegranate
> 8 walnuts, shelled and chopped
> sweet white or red wine

Soak the wheat in cold water for 12 hours. Drain, wash, and cover with fresh cold water. Bring to the boil, then drain and wash through once with cold water. Mix in the sugar and chocolate. Remove all the fruity seeds from the pomegranate and mix them in, then add the walnuts and enough wine to make a smooth mixture. Serve chilled for a delicious and nourishing dessert.

Serves 4

STRANGOLAPRETI FRITTI · FRIED PRIEST STRANGLERS

Just in case the priest didn't choke on the pasta dish, they have another go with the deep-fried version!

> **300 g/10 oz plain white flour**
> **pinch of salt**
> **grated rind of 1 lemon**
> **3 eggs**
> **oil for deep frying**
> **icing sugar for dusting**

Put the flour on to the table and make a hole in it with your fist. Put the salt and lemon rind into the hole, break in the eggs and knead together for a few minutes until smooth. Put the dough into a bowl, cover with a napkin and leave to rest for about 30 minutes. Then break the dough up into pieces and roll each piece out like a breadstick, no thicker. Cut each 'breadstick' into 2–3 cm/ ¾–1¼ inch lengths. Turn a small wicker basket upside down on the table. Take each little piece of dough and push it down on the basket with your thumb so that you end up with a scooped side against your thumb and a lined and grooved side against the basket. Heat the oil and fry the 'priest stranglers' a few at a time. Scoop them out with a slotted spoon when they are crisp and golden, drain on kitchen paper and dust with a little icing sugar. Serve warm with ice-cold sweet wine.

Makes 30–40

FRITTELLE ALLA LUCANA · LUCANIAN FRITTERS

750 ml/1¼ pints cold water
3 tablespoons olive oil
pinch of salt
1 bay leaf
375 g/12 oz plain white flour
30 g/1¼ oz semolina
oil for deep frying
icing sugar for dusting

Put the cold water into a saucepan with the olive oil, salt and bay leaf. Bring to the boil, then tip in the flour and semolina all at once. Remove from the heat and stir energetically with a wooden spoon until the ingredients are thoroughly combined. Return to the heat, and stir until the mixture comes away from the sides of the pan and is smooth and compact. Remove the bay leaf and tip the dough out on to a tray. Smooth it out evenly and leave to cool down, then cut into squares or oblongs. Heat the oil and deep fry the fritters in batches of four or five, pulling at them with a fork as they fry to create a rough surface. When they are puffy and golden, remove from the oil with a slotted spoon and drain on kitchen paper. Dust with icing sugar and serve hot.

Makes 40

TORTA DI LATTICINI ALLA LUCANA · LUCANIAN SAVOURY CHEESECAKE

Very much a special occasion savoury cake with a great many more ingredients than is usual. Like many puddings made in the south, there is an unusual combination of sweet and savoury. The end result is a rich cheesecake, with all the individual flavours of the cheeses.

400 g/13 oz plain white flour
7 egg yolks
200 g/7 oz butter, softened and cubed
200 g/7 oz caster sugar
625 g/1 lb 4 oz fresh Ricotta cheese
50 g/2 oz granulated sugar
2 Mozzarella cheeses, chopped
175 g/6 oz ham, chopped
175 g/6 oz Bel Paese cheese, cubed
40 g/1½ oz Pecorino cheese, grated
2 eggs
salt and pepper
olive oil for greasing

Put the flour on to the table and make a hole in the centre with your fist. Put 4 of the egg yolks, the butter and caster sugar into the hole and knead very lightly, just enough to bind together. Put the dough into a bowl, cover with a clean napkin and leave to rest. Meanwhile, push the Ricotta through a sieve and mix with the granulated sugar, Mozzarella, ham, Bel Paese, Pecorino, eggs and 2 of the remaining egg yolks. This is easiest done by hand, even if it is a little messy. Season with salt and pepper. Roll out half the pastry dough and use to line a greased 30 cm/12 inch cake tin. Fill with the Ricotta mixture, then roll out the rest of the pastry and cover the filled pastry case. Pinch all the edges together and brush with the remaining egg yolk mixed with a little water. Bake in a cool oven (150°C, 300°F, Gas Mark 2) for 1 hour. Serve hot or cold.

Serves 4–6

THE WINES OF BASILICATA

Aglianico del Vulture The best known of Basilicata's very few wines, this is produced in the province of Potenza and apparently has Greek origins. There is another kind of Aglianico produced in the province of Matera known as Aglianico del Colli Lucani. Sometimes the wine is a spumante and is often considered special enough to be subdivided into *Vecchio* and *Riseiva* versions. It has a brilliant red colour, tending towards garnet with a natural foam on the surface, a violet bouquet and a frank, full, rich taste. It is not unlike some of the more refined bottles of Barbera, thus making it a table wine which goes best of all with strong-tasting meat dishes, game, and well-matured cheeses.

Malvasia del Vulture A naturally sparkling golden wine with a faint almond flavour. Excellent as a table wine with all kinds of seafood and fish, egg dishes and some more delicately sauced pasta dishes.

Moscato del Vulture This is produced in a very small area in the province of Potenza with pure Muscat grapes. It has a lovely yellow colour, a delicate bouquet and a velvety, foamy flavour. It is a dessert wine to drink with the delicious fruit and pastries of the region.

Also produced all over the area is the Aspino or Asprinio wine so popular in Campania as a thirst quencher or aperitif. This is essentially a light, refreshing wine with a greenish colour and natural fizz which makes it perfect for drinking in the southern heat.

· CALABRIA ·

The toe of the boot, that's Calabria. The southernmost tip of the Peninsula, it seems to be arrogantly kicking Sicily out into the sapphire-blue sea, and indeed the gesture is reminiscent of the strong, independent Calabrian spirit.

Calabria is a mixture of high, rocky mountains, which are often covered in snow in the winter months, and a fantastic coastline with sandy beaches and rocky bays. The sea embraces the region on three sides; on the west there is the Tyrrhenian Sea and on the east the Ionian laps the coast. Although it is the most rainy of the southern provinces, Calabria has an ideal climate of gentle winters and hot summers cooled by the sea breezes.

The Sila, also known as the great forest of Italy, is the heart of Calabria, and dominates the landscape on the mountains. It is studded with artificial lakes, created by the dams and canals that have brought water and electric power to this dry area. The lakes are icy cold and clear, filled with huge and delicious trout. The Sila is inhabited by all sorts of wild animals, including wolves and wild boar. To the north, the Pollino mountain rises up fiercely to a maximum height of 2,200 metres. The top of the mountain is called *Serra Dolcedorme* (sweetsleeper) but, being totally devoid of vegetation, it is anything but sweet. A long valley separates Pollino from the lovely Sila and then to the south comes the third of Calabria's mountains. This is actually a small range of mountains that falls away towards the sea, called the Serre. But it is up in the tiny villages and hamlets of Sila that all the ancient values and traditions of Calabrian life are preserved from generation to generation.

The rivers of Calabria are many, but they are very short and flow directly down from the mountains into the nearby sea. This means that in winter when the mountain snow melts, the valleys and plains between the mountains and the coastline are often flooded as the swollen rivers burst their banks and rob the farmers of valuable land by smearing acres of it with mud. It also means that some parts of Calabria are permanently in danger of landslides during the winter months.

Calabria's coastline curls its way around the peninsula for 180 kilometres. On the western side, because the mountains are so close, it is very rocky, with deep waters and only very small beaches and bays breaking up the steep and craggy rock face. On the eastern coast you'll find a complete contrast; here the water is shallow and the beaches are longer and much more sandy. The plains that stretch between the mountains and the coastline on both sides of the peninsula were until very recently marshes, rife with malaria. These have been restored and drained and now provide most of the region's agricultural industry, growing vines, olive groves, and, of course, bergamot— a plant exclusive to Calabria which is essential in the manufacture of perfumes.

There are no big cities in Calabria, mainly because the landscape is so mountainous. Most people live in large towns or tiny villages. This is a terribly poor region whose population earns one of the lowest average wages in Italy. Many natives emigrate to the north, even as far as highly industrialized countries such as Germany. Often it is the men who go to seek their fortunes, leaving their families behind to cope in the south.

The region is divided into three large provinces. The first of these is Catanzaro. The city of Catanzaro was founded by the Byzantines in the tenth and eleventh centuries; doubtless they chose the site because with its high perch, surrounded by precipices falling away on both sides into deep torrents, it was easily defendable. Nowadays, in order to facilitate access, a long viaduct has been built to lead into the town. The modern side of the town stretches towards the sea, and is a commercial and agricultural centre of some note. Within its provinces, it is worth noting: the little port of Pizzo where tuna fish are caught for canning and export; the ancient township of Vibo Valentia, rich in Greek, Roman and medieval ruins; and the resort of Tropea for a delicious seaside holiday in a relatively unspoilt area.

The second of the main provinces is Cosenza, which is at the centre of the region's most rich and fertile areas. Five centuries before the birth of Christ, Cosenza was the capital city of a people called Bruzi, who inhabited the region until it was taken over by the Greeks. Within the province of Cosenza lies San Giovanni in Fiore, which is the Sila's main township.

The third province of Calabria is that of Reggio Calabria. The town of that name is the most densely populated in Calabria, and is a main port connecting the region directly to Sicily via Messina. The town was almost completely destroyed by earthquakes in 1783 and 1908 and has now been built anew, complete with massive protection against further earthquakes. Within the province lie various industrial complexes, mainly manufacturing olive oil, pasta and bergamot. Scilla, Locri, Siderno and Bagnara Calabra are wonderful resorts and fishing harbours. The main fish caught in these waters are swordfish and tuna.

Calabria relies heavily on local crafts for some of its income, as the agricultural industry is always uncertain and the fishing somewhat limited. The craftwork consists mainly of ceramics, carpets and handmade cloth. The only industrial centre of any relevance is in Crotone where some very small factories work to extract lead and zinc and produce sulphuric acid and chemical fertilizers.

There is a strictness about Calabrian food, which like its people tends to be lean, austere and simple. The ancient cooking methods of skillet, grill and spit are favoured down here. Yet is it really as simple as it appears at first glance? If you look around you'll see black-clothed women patiently winding dough to make pasta of many shapes and sizes, wielding a willow branch or knitting needle like their mothers and grandmothers before them. The pasta is something they are rightfully proud of in Calabria. The fusilli, fishchietti, ricci di donna, paternoster and many others are still handmade, retaining that rough taste of harsh wheat even through the generous handfuls of Pecorino that are grated over it.

In Calabria the pig is king. Allowed to trundle freely through the village streets, this black, stubborn porker with all its little ones following after it roams at will throughout the summer

months; the whole family lovingly cares for the pig. Then comes
the slaughter, celebrated with great pomp and circumstance in
the autumn with a huge fry up, to which all the family and friends
are invited – often an entire village. At this feast, the best parts of
the pig are fried over an open fire and served with olives, bay
leaves and local herbs. Huge quantities of onions are fried with
the meat and also the justly famous peppers and aubergines,
which every Italian will tell you grow in Calabria as they grow
nowhere else. The peppers in particular are so fleshy, sweet and
juicy as to be almost obscene! They are exported all over Italy.
But back to the feast. Once the celebrations are over, the pig is
turned into all sorts of *salumi* (preserved meats) to keep the
family going through the winter months and into the next summer. They even make the region's most famous sweet-cured
pork. It is a sweet sausage of pig's blood and sugar flavoured
with chocolate. Apart from that, they make many different kinds
of superb cured meats. The sausages are perfection itself when
skewered on to bay tree branches and grilled slowly on a wood
fire.

If you are exploring Calabria, you will find yourself in lovely
Sila before long. Here you will come across some of the most
delicious cheeses you have ever tasted. Always served with the
harsh local bread, they can be eaten for breakfast, lunch, tea or
dinner. Look out for the Butirro, with its rough, stringy crust which
reveals a rich, creamy, fat cheese when cut open. Taste them all,
with their flavour of cold winter days and grasslands warmed by
the sun. Try Rinusu, Tuma, Impanata, and the now world-famous
Caciocavallo. Up in the tiny Sila villages you'll also come across
fabulous huge trout from crystalline lakes. They are cooked very
simply on a red-hot griddle with just a spraying of olive oil and
lemon juice. Then there's the famous and unique *macco di fava*
(recipe on p. 144), a soup made with broad beans and flavoured
with olive oil and masses of freshly ground black pepper.

Not to be forgotten is the lovely Calabrian pizza, called *pitta*
(recipe on p. 149), which is usually dough, spread with a filling,
then rolled up instead of the classical flat circle or square of

dough with a topping. Inside your delicious *pitta* you could find Ricotta and ham, or tuna fish with garlic and black olives, or pork fat with raisins.

Other dishes that should be looked out for in Calabria are the *riso in tortiera* (recipe on p. 151) – risotto with meatballs, tomatoes, Mozzarella and Pecorino; the superbly rich, full-to-bursting *sagne chine* (recipe on p. 147), the local version of lasagne; *schiaffettoni* (recipe on p. 146) – vast stuffed macaroni; all the delicious soups, salads, vegetable stews, pig and mutton dishes, and an imaginative selection of cakes and biscuits.

LE MINESTRE · SOUPS

MACCO DI FAVA · BROAD BEAN AND SPAGHETTI SOUP

A delicious and very traditional broad bean soup served with plenty of freshly ground black pepper and freshly grated Pecorino.

> **200 g/7 oz dried broad beans**
> **1 onion, finely chopped**
> **1 large, very ripe tomato or two small ones, skinned, deseeded and chopped**
> **pinch of sugar**
> **200 g/7 oz spaghetti, broken up into small pieces**
> **85 ml/3 fl oz olive oil**
> **freshly ground black pepper**
> **grated Pecorino cheese**

Soak the beans overnight in plenty of fresh water. Next morning, drain and peel the beans, rinse and place in a saucepan. Cover with 1 litre/1¾ pints salted water and add the onion, tomato and sugar. Cover with a tight-fitting lid and cook on a moderate heat until the beans are tender. Cook the spaghetti separately in a large pan of boiling, salted water then add to the beans with the oil. Stir together very thoroughly, add pepper and Pecorino to taste and serve at once.

Serves 4

LICURDIA · SPRING ONION SOUP

> **1 kg/2 lb spring onions, peeled and coarsely chopped**
> **30 g/1¼ oz pork dripping**

250 g/8 oz stale bread, sliced and toasted
dried red chilli peppers to taste
grated Pecorino cheese

Bring the onions to the boil in 2 litres/3½ pints of salted water with the dripping. Stir together and cook gently for about 1 hour. Meanwhile, rub the toast with the chilli peppers – as little or as much as desired. Lay the flavoured toast in a soup tureen and pour the hot soup over. Sprinkle with plenty of grated cheese and serve at once.

Serves 4

PASTA · PASTA

VERMICELLI AI FUNGHI · VERMICELLI WITH MUSHROOMS

This is a wonderful, simple dish of pasta with fresh mushrooms – the more flavoursome the better, so wild ones are best.

75 g/3 oz lard
1 small onion, chopped
fistful of fresh parsley, chopped
300 g/10 oz tinned tomatoes
300 g/10 oz fresh mushrooms, cleaned and finely chopped
salt
400 g/13 oz vermicelli
grated Pecorino cheese

Mix the lard, onion and parsley together to a paste. Fry gently until the onion is soft but not coloured, then add the tinned tomatoes and simmer for about 10 minutes. Add the mushrooms, season with salt and cook for a further 30 minutes. Boil the vermicelli in plenty of salted water, drain when tender and transfer to a serving dish. Pour over the mushroom sauce, toss together, add plenty of Pecorino and toss again before serving.

Serves 4

SCHIAFFETTONI · STUFFED CANNELLONI

325 g/11 oz dried cannelloni tubes
50 ml/2 fl oz olive oil
325 g/11 oz minced beef
125 g/4 oz salame, diced
150 g/5 oz raw Italian sausage, diced
3 tablespoons water
2 eggs, hardboiled, shelled and chopped
50 g/2 oz butter
75 g/3 oz Pecorino cheese, grated

Boil the cannelloni in plenty of salted water – about 4 at a time. Remove with a large slotted spoon as soon as they are cooked and leave to dry on a damp tablecloth. Meanwhile fry the olive oil, beef, salame and sausage together until well browned, adding the water gradually to give the dish moisture. Strain through a fine sieve to dry it out, and mix with the hardboiled eggs. Reserve any liquid. Stuff each cannelloni tube with the meat and hardboiled egg mixture. Use the butter to grease an ovenproof dish very thoroughly, then arrange the stuffed cannelloni in it in layers, trickling some of the strained liquid on top as you fill the dish. Cover with the grated cheese and bake for 20 minutes in a preheated moderate oven (180°C, 350°F, Gas Mark 4). Serve at once.

Serves 4

SAGNE CHINE · STUFFED LASAGNE

This is a Calabrian version of a classic baked lasagne.

FOR THE PASTA
500 g/1 lb strong white bread flour
salt
about 8 tablespoons water
or
500 g/1 lb readymade lasagne sheets (fresh or dry)

FOR THE FILLING
425 g/14 oz small pork chops or cutlets
200 g/7 oz minced pork
2 tablespoons olive oil
9 tablespoons grated Pecorino cheese
1 egg, beaten
salt and pepper
oil for deep frying
2 tablespoons butter
1 onion, peeled and chopped
1 celery stick, finely chopped
325 g/11 oz mushrooms, peeled and sliced
3 artichoke hearts, thinly sliced
500 g/1 lb fresh peas (shelled weight) or frozen petit pois
3 hardboiled eggs, shelled and sliced
1 Mozzarella, thinly sliced
4 tablespoons passata or sieved canned tomatoes

If making your own pasta, blend the flour and salt with enough water to make a fairly stiff dough. Knead until smooth, then leave to rest for about 30 minutes. Roll it out several times, cut into oblongs and boil, 3 pieces at a time, for about 3 minutes. Drain carefully and lay out on a damp cloth until required. If using readymade pasta, boil until *al dente*, drain and lay out as above.

Fry the chops and minced pork in the olive oil until the meat is well browned. Remove the chops from the pan, take the meat off the bone and cube it, then set aside. Stir 3 tablespoons Pecorino, the beaten egg and seasoning into the minced pork. Remove from the heat and roll into small meatballs. Deep fry in hot oil until crisp, then drain and set aside.

Fry the butter, onion and celery together until the onion is soft, then add the mushrooms, artichoke hearts and peas. Stir, season, then simmer until cooked through. Oil a deep ovenproof dish and layer the pasta with the meatballs, cooked vegetables, sliced hardboiled eggs, cubed pork chop meat and Mozzarella between each layer. Finish off with the passata and the remaining Pecorino. Bake in a preheated moderate oven (180°C, 350°F, Gas Mark 4) for 30 minutes.

Serves 6–8

PASTA E ARROSTO · PASTA WITH ROAST MEAT AND QUAILS

Various kinds of meat can be added to this ancient dish of pasta and roast meat. In this original recipe pork and quails are used.

> **200 g/7 oz roasting pork (loin or leg)**
> **200 g/7 oz roasting goat or mutton**
> **4 quails, ready to roast**
> **125 ml/4 fl oz olive oil**
> **salt and pepper**
> **fresh or dried rosemary and sage**
> **glass of red wine**
> **300 g/10 oz vermicelli or other pasta**

Put the pork, goat or mutton, and quails in a roasting tin. Coat with the olive oil, season, and sprinkle with the herbs. Roast in a preheated moderate oven (180°C, 350°F, Gas Mark 4) for about

30 minutes or until cooked through, basting occasionally with the red wine. When the meat is cooked, remove the juices from the tin and strain into a frying pan. Mince the pork and goat or mutton and keep the quails hot in the oven. Mix the minced meat up with the juices in the frying pan and keep hot whilst you cook the pasta in plenty of boiling salted water. When the pasta is *al dente*, drain and add to the pan with the minced meat. Toss quickly over a hot flame to combine, then transfer to a serving platter. Arrange the quails on top and serve.

Serves 4

PITTA CON PANCETTA E UVETTA · PITTA WITH BACON AND SULTANAS

You could also fill this pitta with sun-dried tomatoes and plenty of oregano – or see p. 150 for other suggestions.

> **500 g/1 lb bread dough, fully risen (see basic recipe on page 218)**
> **8 tablespoons olive oil**
> **250 g/8 oz streaky bacon, coarsely chopped**
> **250 g/8 oz sultanas, soaked in warm water for 15 minutes then drained and dried**

Place the dough on the table and knead with half the oil. Work it thoroughly for about 15 minutes, then push it flat with your hands until it is about 5 cm/2 inches thick, forming a wide rectangle. Cover with the bacon and sultanas and roll up to make a cylinder. Bend it into a ring and place an oiled metal bowl in the middle of the ring to keep the shape. Place the ring and the bowl on an oiled baking sheet and bake in a preheated moderate oven (180°C, 350°F, Gas Mark 4) for about 1 hour.

Serves 6–8

PIZZA · PIZZA

PIZZA CON LA RICOTTA · PIZZA WITH A RICOTTA FILLING

This pizza is made with the Ricotta, ham and egg filling safely tucked inside two sheets of dough.

> **500 g/1 lb flour**
> **20 g/¾ oz fresh yeast, diluted to a smooth paste in a little warm water**
> **4 tablespoons olive oil**
> **pinch of salt**
> **4 tablespoons milk**
> **250 g/8 oz freshest Ricotta cheese, crumbled into small pieces**
> **125 g/4 oz Calabrian sausage or prosciutto crudo (Parma ham), chopped**
> **50 g/2 oz Pecorino cheese, freshly grated**
> **2 eggs, hardboiled and chopped**
> **chopped fresh parsley**
> **salt and pepper**
> **a little lard**

Make a dough with the flour, yeast, olive oil, salt and enough of the milk to make it manageable. Knead carefully and thoroughly as though you were making bread. Leave to rise in a warm place for about 1 hour or until doubled in size. Then divide into two pieces. Oil a very large flat cake or flan tin and roll out half the dough to cover the bottom. Spread the Ricotta, sausage or prosciutto, Pecorino, chopped hardboiled eggs and parsley all over the dough as evenly as possible. Season with salt and pepper. Roll out the second piece of dough, cover the filling and pinch the edges together carefully all around. Pierce the top of the pizza all over with a fork, then dot with a few flakes of lard. Place in a preheated moderate oven (180°C, 350°F, Gas Mark 4) for about 30 minutes or until the pizza is crisp and golden on the surface. Serve hot or cold.

Serves 4–6

IL RISO · RICE

RISO IN TORTIERA · BAKED RICE TIMBALE

This is one of the very few long and complicated dishes in Calabrian cookery. It's a superb dish of rice with tiny meatballs, Mozzarella and eggs, baked in the oven.

1 raw egg
approximately 3 tablespoons fresh breadcrumbs
olive oil for frying
500 g/1 lb risotto rice
4 hardboiled eggs, sliced
200 g/7 oz Mozzarella cheese, sliced
125 g/4 oz Pecorino cheese, grated, plus an extra 2
level tablespoons
salt

FOR THE SAUCE
1 onion, finely chopped
125 ml/4 fl oz olive oil
250 g/8 oz shin of beef
½ glass red wine
500 g/1 lb tinned tomatoes
few fresh basil leaves

2 tablespoons tomato paste
salt

Make the sauce first: using a terracotta pan if you have one, fry the onion gently in the olive oil until it is soft but not coloured. Then add the shin of beef and brown thoroughly on all sides. Add the wine, raise the heat to evaporate the fumes, then lower the heat and add the tomatoes, basil, tomato paste and salt. Cook gently under a lid until the meat is cooked through, adding a little hot water from time to time – you need a large quantity of sauce.

When the meat is falling apart, remove and cut in half. Chop one half coarsely and return to the sauce. Mince the other piece finely, place in a bowl and mix with the raw egg and 1 tablespoon fresh breadcrumbs. If the mixture is too soft, add a few more breadcrumbs or some of the grated cheese. Form into tiny meatballs about the size of a hazelnut. Fry in oil and drain on paper.

Boil the rice in a large pan of salted water until tender. Drain, place in a bowl, and dress with about half the tomato and meat sauce. Grease an ovenproof dish and spread half the dressed rice across the bottom, smoothing the surface with a spatula. Place half of the hardboiled eggs, Mozzarella, Pecorino, meatballs and tomato sauce on top. Cover with the rest of the rice, then put all the remaining ingredients on top of that. Dribble a little olive oil over the dish, cover with a thin coating of the remaining breadcrumbs and grated Pecorino. Place in a hot oven (200°C, 400°F, Gas Mark 6) for about fifteen minutes or until the top is crisp and golden, then serve.

Serves 6–8

I LEGUMI · VEGETABLES

CIAMBOTTA · VEGETABLE CASSEROLE

Calabria is famous for its peppers, and in this delicious vegetable stew they are put to excellent use. Aubergines feature strongly in local dishes too; the eggplant is the most widely cultivated plant in the whole of southern Italy.

>   1 large onion, coarsely chopped
>   olive oil
>   2 large peppers, any colour, blanched, skinned and
>   sliced
>   2–3 potatoes, peeled and cut into quarters
>   3 medium-sized aubergines, peeled and thickly sliced
>   3 celery sticks, cut into chunks
>   6 green olives
>   salt

Fry the onion in olive oil until browned, then add all the other vegetables and the olives. Cook until the vegetables are tender, stirring frequently. Season to taste with salt. Serve warm.

Serves 4–6

CONTORNO PER IL PESCE · SALAD TO SERVE WITH BOILED OR ROAST FISH

This very simple potato salad is Calabria's traditional accompaniment to all kinds of fish dishes, hot or cold.

>   10 new potatoes
>   4 eggs

7 pickled onions, chopped
1 heaped tablespoon capers, washed
5 tablespoons best-quality olive oil
salt

Boil the potatoes until tender and hardboil the eggs. Slice the potatoes and eggs to roughly the same size. Slice the onions into small pieces. Mix the potatoes, eggs, onions and capers together. Stir in the oil and salt and serve with any fish dish.

Serves 4

INSALATA CALABRESE · CALABRIAN SALAD

The inhabitants of this region are very fond of salads but they never use anything sour like vinegar or lemon juice in the dressing, just plenty of good olive oil.

4 large potatoes
2 large onions, thinly sliced
3 green peppers, deseeded and thinly sliced
salt
6 tablespoons best-quality olive oil

Bake the potatoes in their jackets, then peel and slice into a salad bowl while still warm. Add the sliced onions and peppers and mix together. Dress with salt and the olive oil and serve.

Serves 4

I PESCI · FISH

TORTIERA DI SARDINE · BAKED SARDINES

800 g/1 lb 10 oz fresh sardines
50 g/2 oz Pecorino cheese, freshly grated
75 g/3 oz stale white bread, grated
pinch of dried oregano
2 cloves garlic, finely sliced
small fistful of fresh parsley, chopped
pinch of salt
8 tablespoons olive oil
3 ripe fresh tomatoes, washed and sliced

Open the sardines up, remove the guts and the head. Pull out the central bone with care so as not to tear the fish, then close up again. Mix the grated Pecorino with the grated bread. Stir in the oregano, garlic, parsley and salt. Use some of the oil to grease an ovenproof dish thoroughly and scatter enough of the bread mixture across the bottom to cover it completely. Arrange a layer of fish on top and cover with more of the bread mixture. Cover with another layer of fish and then the remaining bread mixture. Arrange the sliced tomatoes on top, dribble over the rest of the oil and bake in a preheated moderate oven (180°C, 350°F, Gas Mark 4) for 30 minutes. Serve hot or cold.

Serves 4

ALICI A BECCAFICO · STUFFED FRIED SARDINES

A delicious way to serve fresh sardines.

8 fresh sardines
1 glass dry white wine

50 g/2 oz fresh breadcrumbs
30 g/1¼ oz Pecorino cheese, freshly grated
2 tablespoons chopped fresh parsley
large pinch of dried oregano
1 clove garlic, peeled and finely chopped
1 tablespoon olive oil
3 level tablespoons plain white flour
oil for deep frying
4 tablespoons plain tomato sauce
1 lemon, quartered, to garnish

Open out the sardines and remove the heads and central spines without splitting or breaking the fish. Lay them in the wine and leave to soak while you prepare the filling.

Blend the breadcrumbs with the cheese, parsley, oregano, garlic and olive oil. Spread this mixture on 4 fish and use the other 4 to cover the stuffing completely. Secure with wooden cocktail sticks if necessary. Toss each one in the flour and deep fry in hot oil until golden and crisp. Drain on paper and serve with the tomato sauce and lemon wedges.

Serves 4

PESCE STOCCO ALLA CALABRESE · CALABRIAN STOCKFISH STEW

1 large onion, finely chopped
fistful of fresh parsley, finely chopped
125 ml/4 fl oz olive oil
1 heaped tablespoon tomato paste
1 ladleful hot fish stock or boiling water
800 g/1 lb 10 oz dried salt cod (stockfish), soaked overnight
800 g/1 lb 10 oz potatoes, peeled

sprig of fresh basil
125 g/4 oz black olives, stoned
pinch of salt
pinch of white pepper

Put the onion, parsley and oil into a heavy pan, preferably
terracotta, and fry gently together for a few minutes. Stir in the
tomato paste, then cook until the oil is beginning to separate
from the tomato. Add the fish stock or water, stir and continue to
cook for a little longer. Meanwhile, boil the salt cod for about 10
minutes in plenty of water; drain and remove the skin and bones,
being careful not to break up the fish. Cut into neat sections and
add to the tomato sauce. Slice the potatoes ½ cm/¼ inch thick
and add to the pan. Add the basil and cover. Cook until the
potatoes are just tender, then add the olives and seasoning.
Remove from the heat and leave to stand, covered, for 10
minutes before serving.

Serves 4

TONNO LESSATO · POACHED TUNA

This is one of my favourite ways of eating fish – cooked very
simply, retaining all the freshness of the flavour and preserving
the texture.

1 carrot, scraped
1 onion, peeled and quartered
1 celery stick, quartered
2 bay leaves
salt
750 g/1½ lb fresh tuna (in one piece)
50 g/2 oz fresh parsley, chopped
2 cloves garlic, peeled and chopped

4 tablespoons olive oil
freshly ground black pepper

Place the carrot, onion, celery and bay leaves in a deep sauce-pan with about 2 litres/3½ pints cold water and a large pinch of salt. Bring to the boil and simmer for about 45 minutes. Tie the fish up with string so it won't fall apart in the cooking, then lay it in the stock and poach for about 15 minutes, depending upon its thickness. Mix the parsley and garlic together. When the fish is cooked, remove from the stock, discard the string, and slice into 4. Arrange the fish on a platter and sprinkle the parsley and garlic over, then drizzle the oil over that and grind on plenty of black pepper. Serve hot or cold.

Serves 4

TONNO IN AGRODOLCE · SWEET AND SOUR TUNA

A sweet and sour dish made with fresh tuna. Often the alalonga fish is used instead of the larger tuna. Alalonga is a white-fleshed, small tuna whose meat is much more expensive than ordinary tuna.

700 g/1 lb 7 oz fresh or frozen tuna steaks
3 level tablespoons plain white flour
oil for deep frying
2 large onions, sliced
½ glass red wine vinegar
1 level tablespoon sugar
salt

Cut the tuna into neat squares and toss them in the flour. Heat the oil and fry the tuna quickly, turning it so it doesn't become too brown. Remove and leave to drain in a warm place. In the remaining oil, fry the onions. During the cooking sprinkle over the vinegar and sugar. Season with a little salt. When the onions are soft, arrange the fried tuna amongst the onions and heat through. Arrange on a dish and serve at once.

Serves 4

LE CARNI · MEAT

COSTOLETTE D'AGNELLO ALLA CALABRESE · CALABRIAN LAMB CUTLETS

Very little meat is cooked in Calabria; what there is is almost always either pork or mutton, like this delicious dish of lamb cutlets with tomatoes, olives, peppers and other strong southern flavours.

> **700 g/1 lb 7 oz lamb cutlets, as small and neat as possible**
> **125 ml/4 fl oz olive oil**
> **1 small onion, chopped**
> **500 g/1 lb tinned tomatoes or ripe, fresh tomatoes, chopped**
> **fistful of fresh parsley, chopped**
> **125 g/4 oz green olives**
> **2 peppers, preferably yellow, red or one of each, blanched, skinned and thinly sliced**
> **pinch of mixed spices**
> **salt**

Fry the lamb cutlets in half the olive oil. In a separate pan, fry the onion gently in the remaining oil, then add the tomatoes, parsley, olives, peppers, mixed spices and salt. Stir it all together and simmer gently until cooked (about 30 minutes). Add the cutlets to the sauce with their juices. Season carefully, heat through and serve at once with plenty of bread to mop up the sauce.

Serves 4

CARNE ALLA PECORARA · SHEPHERD'S LAMB

> **625 g/1 lb 4 oz lamb (or use veal or chicken), boned and cut into chunks**
> **125 ml/4 fl oz olive oil**
> **4 cloves garlic, thinly sliced**
> **large pinch of dried oregano**
> **6 ripe tomatoes, peeled, deseeded and finely chopped**
> **salt and pepper**

Put the meat in a casserole dish with the oil, garlic, oregano and tomatoes. Season with salt and pepper. Cover and simmer very slowly over a low heat until a thick sauce has formed around the meat – about 1½ hours. Baste occasionally with a little water if required. Serve hot.

Serves 6

I DOLCI · DESSERTS, PIES AND PASTRIES

NEPITELLE · CHOCOLATE TARTS

Also called *pittapie* or *pitte nepite*. These are delicious and intricate little pastries linked with household festivities and

Christmas time. They are widely available for sale in the *pasticcerie* of the region but are great fun and even better when made at home.

> 500 g/1 lb plain white flour
> 125 g/4 oz butter or margarine
> 125 g/4 oz sugar
> grated rind of 1 lemon
> 3 eggs
> 250 g/8 oz sultanas, soaked in warm water for 15 minutes
> 50 g/2 oz chocolate, grated
> 50 g/2 oz almonds, blanched and chopped
> a little sweet wine
> fat for greasing
> a little cinnamon

Mix the flour with the butter or margarine, half the sugar, the lemon rind and the eggs and knead to a smooth, compact dough. Roll out to a disc 1 cm/½ inch thick and then cut into 7.5 cm/3 inch circles with a glass. Roll out the trimmings and cut into strips. Drain the sultanas and mix with the chocolate, the rest of the sugar and the almonds, using a little sweet wine to help it all stick together, then spoon this mixture on to each circle of dough. Pull the edges up around the filling and decorate the top with the strips of dough in a lattice pattern. Grease a baking sheet and place the tarts on it. Sprinkle with cinnamon then bake in a cool oven (150°C, 300°F, Gas Mark 2) for 30 minutes. Serve cold.

Serves 6

SAMMARTINA · ALMOND, WALNUT AND SULTANA FLAN

> **500 g/1 lb plain white flour**
> **250 g/8 oz butter**
> **250 g/8 oz sugar**
> **5 eggs**
> **grated rind of 1 lemon**
> **salt**
> **butter for greasing**
> **150 g/5 oz almonds, blanched and chopped**
> **150 g/5 oz walnuts, peeled and chopped**
> **125 g/4 oz sultanas, soaked in water for 15 minutes**
> **then drained**
> **a little sweet wine**

Mix the flour, butter, sugar, eggs, lemon rind and salt together to make a rich pastry. Leave to rest for 30 minutes then butter a 30 cm/12 inch flan case and line with the rolled-out pastry. Mix the almonds, walnuts and sultanas with a little sweet wine and scatter them over the pastry case. Press them into the dough and bake in a preheated moderate oven (180°C, 350°F, Gas Mark 4) until golden brown – about 30 minutes. Serve hot or cold.

Serves 8

UOVA ALLA MONACELLA · LITTLE NUNS' EGGS

This dish appears in Calabria in two completely different versions. This is the sweet version, made with cocoa, cinnamon and sugar. The savoury version makes a very simple starter – hard-boiled eggs, sliced in half and laid in an ovenproof dish, then covered with a very piquant tomato sauce.

> **6 eggs, hardboiled**

125 g/4 oz sweet cocoa powder or drinking chocolate,
sifted
75 g/3 oz icing sugar, sifted
2 large pinches powdered cinnamon
1 egg yolk
oil for deep frying
1 egg white, whisked until foamy

Cool and shell the eggs, cut them in half and push the yolks
through a sieve. Mix half the cocoa powder into the sieved egg
yolks with the sugar and 1 pinch of cinnamon. Blend the raw egg
yolk into this mixture and stuff the 12 egg white halves with it.
Heat the oil until sizzling. Dip the stuffed egg whites into the
remaining cocoa mixed with the cinnamon. Then dip into the
whisked egg white to coat completely. Deep fry in the oil for
about 6 minutes, then drain carefully and serve hot.

Serves 4–6

TURTIDDI · HOT HONEY CAKES

These are sweet gnocchi made for Christmas feasts. Locally, they
believe that making sweet fried pastries and goodies will bring
you good luck around Christmas time. Only those families who
are in mourning do not participate in the frying of batches of
these and other sweets, and it is up to the friends of the bereaved
to send parcels of cakes to the households where it is not
permitted to fry.

500 g/1 lb fine plain white flour
125 g/4 oz best olive oil
250 ml/8 fl oz sweet white wine, preferably Moscato
juice and grated rind of 1 orange
pinch of cinnamon

oil for deep frying
150 g/5 oz best honey

Mix the flour with the olive oil, wine, orange rind and cinnamon. Knead until smooth and then roll out like a snake. Cut off small chunks and roll these over a grater or the back of a fork so that one side is dented and the other side grooved – like making gnocchi. Deep fry in hot oil for about 5 minutes. Meanwhile heat the honey and orange juice, mixing constantly until you have a boiling and smooth amalgam. Drain the gnocchi and transfer to the honey mixture, keeping off the heat. Stir to mix, then lift out with forks, place on to plates and serve at once.

Serves 4

CANNARICULI · CHRISTMAS FRITTERS

This is my own adaptation of Calabria's best-loved Christmas speciality. They are very easy to make and rather sticky.

200 g/7 oz fine plain white flour
about 125 ml/4 fl oz very sweet wine
oil for deep frying (preferably olive oil)
150 ml/5 fl oz liquid honey
5 tablespoons water
50 g/2 oz sugar crystals

Mix the flour and wine together until a dough of about the same texture as bread dough is formed. Roll the dough into thick pencil shapes. Heat the oil until sizzling hot, then fry the *cannariculi* until golden and crisp. Melt the honey with the water over a low heat until just boiling. Drop the fritters into the melted honey to cover them, then take them out and arrange in a dish. Decorate with the sugar crystals before serving.

Makes about 20

THE WINES OF CALABRIA

The wines of this severe, stern region have roots that wind their way back in time to the point where history becomes legend. All the wines are typical of Calabria's unique personality, dry and austere yet full and generous at the same time. The reds are all luscious and sexy, the whites are either clean and dry, or deep, dark coloured and sweetly lusty.

The wines of southern Italy generally have a reputation for being somewhat sweeter and less refined than the wines of the north, but recent efforts are changing all this and local producers are contributing more and more to the excellent variety of wines that Italy exports worldwide.

Ciro This was drunk during the earliest Olympic Games to give the athletes energy and power and is produced in the province of Cosenza to this very day, probably fairly unchanged. Ciro Rosso is a superior table wine, especially good with roast meat and the local game dishes. The white version is most likely to be the older variety and has the slightly rounded, sweetish flavour that was so much favoured in times gone by. It has a straw-yellow colour and a very heady nose, and is delicious with heavily sauced fish dishes.

Greco di Gerace Another very old local white wine, made with grapes that were brought across the water from Greece many centuries ago. It has an unmistakable scent of orange blossom and a rounded, velvety taste. It's a really delicious wine that can be drunk as an aperitif or as a wine to end a special meal. It's very strong, so don't drive if you're imbibing this one.

Moscato di Calabria This is fairly rare and rather special. It is sweet and smooth with a yellow amber colour and the typical nose of a real Muscat wine.

Pollino One of the region's most famous reds, produced with a wide variety of grapes in the area around Castrovillari, Cassano Ionio, San Basile and Civita Francineto. It's a smooth, light-ruby-coloured wine with plenty of body and dryness. Excellent with the local meat dishes and, if aged with care, can become a truly remarkable wine.

Savuto Another typical red wine, with the glorious nickname of *succo di pietra*: stone juice. It has a brilliant, bright, ruby colour and a dry, velvety flavour, and is excellent with all game and roast meats, especially if aged for a few years.

Other wines of the region include: Bianco di Nicastro, Bianco di Squillace, Caronte (red), Lamezia or Lamertino, Melissa (red), Greco di Ponte Grande (red), and Esaro (white).

· SICILY ·

Sicily forms the bridge between the cultures and traditions of northern Africa and the rest of Europe via Italy. It is neither one nor the other, because the passage of time and history has meant that all kinds of races and creeds have stayed here, and have left something of themselves behind. You will find blue-eyed, blond men, with ancient Norman blood flowing through their veins, and short, squat, dark women whose ancestry must be Saracen. For many centuries, the island has been used and abused, appreciated, loved and then scorned. The modern visitor finds Sicily mysterious, dangerous and enticing. Deeply honourable, sunk into its traditions and extraordinary sense of pride and family blood ties, the island can be frightening and deeply disturbing, but you'd have to be made of stone not to be attracted to it. You will always have the strange feeling there that you *cannot* be in control of your destiny; everything has already been decided and there is nothing you can do about it. Everybody is aware of the power behind the beauty, and you'd be very foolish to ignore it or try to fight it. The Mafia started here in the fifteenth century and was originally a secret society which avenged wrongs by means of a vendetta. It is, of course, completely out of hand these days, but the very old values that inspired it to begin with still count for something in Sicily and its influence can still be felt. Crops fail mysteriously overnight, holiday centres somehow never get built, and the deeper inland you go, the more strange the looks you receive. Yet if you ask, they'll tell you there is a reason for everything . . .

Some friends of mine went to live near Agrigento. They are a young couple, very British, with a small daughter called Louise. From the very start they were completely captivated by the island's beauty and atmosphere; they felt stirred and alive, lulled by the sun and the scent of oranges on the breeze. Tom went happily to work at the local English language school and mother and daughter set about making a home in their new surroundings. Jane bought Louise a pet goat, and a chain and a peg to go with it; the animal proceeded to weed their garden for them.

A few months later, a large black car drew up outside the front door one evening towards dusk. Two large men knocked at the door, chewing toothpicks and watching the family through their very dark sunglasses. Their hair was slicked down with oil, and it was as black and shiny as their suits. They stank of cheap cologne and had perfectly manicured hands. Their teeth shone brilliant white in the gloom as they slowly smiled at Tom, who stood very Britishly in his doorway.

The one with a pencil-thin moustache did the talking. In heavily accented American he asked if he might come in and talk to 'the master'. Reluctantly Tom led the way to the kitchen and offered wine. The gist of the conversation was that the visitors wanted to welcome the English family to the area, but they did feel a little worried about strangers living so remotely, and they felt that 50,000 lire per month would adequately pay for the degree of protection required. They were unbearably polite, the Sicilian spoke softly and coolly, but Tom (an Englishman's home is his castle etc. etc.) threw them both out. The next day and all the following week their washing disappeared from their clothes-line, flowers were uprooted from their garden, repairs and deliveries didn't happen, and half the local shopkeepers mysteriously ran out of all the things they needed.

At the end of a fortnight's campaign like this, the goat was taken. At the end of the goat's chain was a note which read, 'The furry thing has gone, the one who loves the furry thing the most will be the next to go'. At this point, British pride was no match for Sicilian honour and Tom made contact with the men through the local café. He paid the 50,000 lire per month regularly and life could not have been simpler and sweeter. All the washing was returned, ironed and folded; the garden was planted with countless new flowers and vegetables; the goat was returned, plump and happy; there were gifts of wine, oil and fruit left on the doorstep; and any repairs needed were carried out instantly and efficiently. Yet the spell had been broken for Jane and Tom and their conscience would not let them rest. To the astonishment and complete bewilderment of their neighbours, they left a year later and have never been back.

Whether you are from Munich or Florence, you will always be a stranger on this island. Being Italian makes no difference, even though the gap across the Strait of Messina measures only three kilometres. And wherever you've just arrived from, Sicily will capture you and spin you into its enchanted web from the first moment.

The island's gastronomy reflects all its cultures and traditions: there are rich ornate Spanish-style dishes; opulent, strange combinations of flavours from Arabia; selective style and good taste from the Normans; deeply religious, symbolic dishes. It is without question an extremely intense style of cooking, very elaborate and almost always very rich. Countless ingredients are used, and each course has its own importance. Take, for example, the original cassata, from the Arab word *quas'at*, which means large round bowl. Cassata found its way to Sicily from Arabia and used to be prepared by nuns in honour of the Easter festivities, until they were banned from doing so in the sixteenth century because the religious powers felt the sisters were spending too much time on the cassata and not enough time on their duties during Holy Week. Nowadays cassata is recognized and enjoyed the world over; who would ever have thought it had such a history?

A great deal of fish is used in this cuisine, and vast amounts of vegetables, but almost no meat at all. There is very little animal fat, and this makes it one of the world's healthiest diets despite its richness and enormous portions. However, it is pasta that is the emblem of this island's culinary scene: pasta dressed with fish, triumphant with countless colourful vegetables, almost never with meat. It is the most baroque style of cooking you will ever see, and after all, are you not surrounded by the baroque churches, palaces, villas, customs and traditions in which the island buries itself? This is a wild, untamed land with a deceptively smooth expression, where the sun shines down inexorably and flavours everything with heat, passion and golden light.

ANTIPASTI · ANTIPASTI

FRITTELLE DI MELANZANE · AUBERGINE FRITTERS

1 kg/2 lb aubergines, thickly sliced
90 g/3½ oz sultanas
2 egg yolks
75 g/3 oz Pecorino cheese, grated
large pinch of dried oregano
¼ teaspoon freshly grated nutmeg
freshly ground black pepper
3 level tablespoons plain white flour
1 egg, beaten
3–4 tablespoons fresh white breadcrumbs
oil for deep frying

Put the sliced aubergines into a saucepan and cover with cold salted water. Put a heavy plate on top and leave for about 45 minutes. Cover the sultanas with water and let them soak also for 45 minutes. Then drain the aubergines and put them back in the saucepan with enough fresh water to cover. Drain and dry the sultanas and set aside. Boil the aubergines for about 5 minutes, then drain. Chop them up as finely as possible (before you start chopping, squeeze out as much water as you can by hand).

Put the chopped aubergines into a bowl and add the sultanas, egg yolks, cheese, oregano, nutmeg and plenty of black pepper. Mix together, then shape into little balls and toss them first in the flour, then the beaten egg, then the breadcrumbs. Heat the oil and fry the fritters until crisp and golden. Drain them on kitchen paper and serve hot or cold as a delicious antipasto.

Makes 24 fritters

ARANCINE DI RISO · FRIED RICE BALLS

These fritters are known as 'little oranges' because that's what they look like. Originally from Sicily they are now popular throughout the country.

3 tablespoons olive oil
75 g/3 oz butter
½ onion, finely chopped
125 g/4 oz chicken livers, finely chopped
125 g/4 oz veal trimmings, finely chopped
150 g/5 oz fresh young peas (shelled weight), or frozen petit pois
1½ tablespoons tomato paste
250 ml/8 fl oz hot chicken broth
fistful of fresh parsley, chopped
fistful of fresh basil, chopped
1 celery stick, chopped
salt and pepper
3 eggs
300 g/10 oz boiling rice
500 ml/17 fl oz cold water
pinch of powdered saffron
3 heaped tablespoons grated Caciocavallo or Parmesan cheese
3 level tablespoons plain white flour
3–4 tablespoons fresh white breadcrumbs
oil for deep frying

Put the olive oil and about a third of the butter in a saucepan with the onion. Fry until the onion is translucent, then add the chicken livers, veal and peas. Cook for about 5 minutes, then dilute the tomato paste in the broth, stir in the chopped herbs and celery, and add to the saucepan. Season, cover and simmer while you prepare the rest of the dish. Hardboil 1 of the eggs, shell and chop finely. Boil the rice in the water with a little salt. Cook until just underdone, then drain, if there is any water left, and stir in the remaining butter, the saffron, cheese and 1 egg. Stir it all together very well, then shape most of the mixture into little round balls. Make a hollow in the centre of each one and fill with a little of the tomato sauce and some chopped hardboiled egg. Cover up the filling with the remaining rice; dip each ball into flour, then into the remaining egg, beaten, then the breadcrumbs. Heat the oil and fry the balls until crisp and golden. Drain on paper and serve.

Serves 6

CACIU ALL'ARGINTERA · SILVERSMITH'S CHEESE

The name derives from a bankrupt silversmith who invented this way of cooking cheese to remind himself of better times when he could still afford to eat meat.

> **300 g/10 oz Caciocavallo cheese**
> **50 ml/2 fl oz olive oil**
> **1 clove garlic, lightly crushed**
> **dried oregano**
> **freshly ground black pepper**
> **salt**

Slice the cheese evenly. Heat the oil in a frying pan with the garlic until very hot and as soon as the garlic is blackened remove it and add the cheese. Fry it gently on both sides, then transfer it to an ovenproof dish. Put in a moderate oven (190°C, 375°F, Gas Mark 5) for about 8 minutes, sprinkle with the oregano, freshly ground black pepper and a little salt. Serve at once.

Serves 4

PASTA · PASTA

ZITE AL POMODORO E TONNO · PASTA WITH TUNA AND TOMATO SAUCE

This is one of the very few reasonably simple and easily digested dishes in the vast range of Sicilian specialities. The tuna fish must be preserved in oil, preferably olive oil, to achieve the correct flavour.

> 400 g/13 oz ripe tomatoes
> 5 tablespoons olive oil
> 1 small onion, chopped
> 1 large clove garlic, chopped
> 2 salted or 3 canned anchovies, filleted and chopped
> 50 g/2 oz canned tuna fish (in oil), flaked
> large pinch of black pepper
> salt
> 325 g/11 oz zite pasta, broken

Chop and deseed the tomatoes without peeling them. Heat the oil and fry the onion and garlic gently, then add the anchovies and cream them with a fork. Simmer for 5 minutes then add the tomatoes. Cover and simmer for 20 minutes, then add the tuna and the black pepper. Taste and adjust the seasoning. Meanwhile, bring a large pot of salted water to the boil, toss in the broken zite and cook until tender. Drain and dress with the sauce before serving.

Serves 4

PASTA 'CHI VROCCULI ARRIMINATI' · PASTA WITH SAUTÉED CAULIFLOWER

This is a real favourite with me. It looks so oriental and spicy. Brilliantly coloured with saffron and the pure-white cauliflower, it is simple and complex at the same time.

> 1 small cauliflower, broken into medium-sized florets
> 1 onion, sliced
> 1 large wine glass olive oil
> pinch of saffron powder, diluted in a little water
> 3 salted or 4 canned anchovies, trimmed and filleted
> 50 g/2 oz currants, washed and dried
> 50 g/2 oz pine kernels
> 325 g/11 oz macaroni
> 2 fistfuls grated Pecorino cheese mixed with 4 fresh basil leaves, chopped

Boil the cauliflower florets in salted water until tender then scoop them out with a slotted spoon. Save the water. Fry the onion in half the oil until translucent, then add the saffron, cover and simmer for about 5 minutes. Add the cauliflower florets. Fry the anchovies in the rest of the oil, mashing the fish with a fork to make it creamy. Add this to the cauliflower with the currants and pine kernels. Boil the macaroni in the cauliflower water, drain, and add to the cauliflower mixture. Add the Pecorino and basil, and mix the whole lot together until all the flavours have had a chance to mingle amongst the pasta, then serve.

Serves 4

PASTA 'CA MUDDICA' · PASTA WITH BREADCRUMBS

Pasta with breadcrumbs, the breadcrumbs replacing the cheese which would otherwise be used. This version is from western Sicily and includes tomatoes, whereas in the east tomatoes are not used in the dish, and the breadcrumbs are toasted in a frying pan over a flame and not in the oven.

> 125 ml/4 fl oz olive oil
> 2 cloves garlic, peeled
> 500 g/1 lb fresh tomatoes, peeled, deseeded and chopped
> fistful of fresh parsley, chopped
> 125 g/4 oz canned or salted anchovies, filleted, washed and chopped
> 125 g/4 oz stale breadcrumbs
> 500 g/1 lb of your favourite pasta shape – penne, wheels or other

Heat two-thirds of the olive oil with the garlic, then when the garlic is golden brown scoop it out and add the tomatoes, parsley and anchovies, mashing the anchovies into the sauce with a fork. Scatter the breadcrumbs into a small ovenproof dish, cover with the remaining oil and toast in the oven. Bring a large pot of salted water to a rolling boil, toss in the pasta, stir, and cook until *al dente*. Drain the pasta, transfer to a warm bowl and dress with the tomato sauce. Toss it all together, scatter the toasted breadcrumbs over and serve.

Serves 4

VERMICELLI ALLA SIRACUSANA · SIRACUSA VERMICELLI

This spectacular dish brings together all the wonders of the island, all the most brilliant colours – deep-purple aubergine, golden-yellow pepper, red tomatoes, green capers and black olives – and the texture and flavours heightened by the ever-present combination of basil, garlic and anchovy.

> **1 sweet yellow pepper, as large as possible**
> **50 ml/2 fl oz olive oil**
> **1 clove garlic, peeled**
> **2 canned or salted anchovies, filleted**
> **1 large aubergine, diced**
> **300 g/10 oz fresh ripe tomatoes, deseeded if preferred, and sliced into strips**
> **8 Sicilian olives, stoned**
> **6 fresh basil leaves, chopped**
> **1 tablespoon capers, washed and chopped**
> **salt**
> **325 g/11 oz vermicelli**
> **grated Caciocavallo or Pecorino cheese**

Put a large pot of salted water on to boil for the pasta. Push a fork through the pepper and singe it over a flame or under a grill; scrape off the outer skin with a small, sharp knife, then cut it open, remove the seeds and inner membrane, and slice it into thin strips. Heat the olive oil with the garlic; when the garlic is golden brown, remove, and add the anchovies. Mash them into the oil with a fork, then add the aubergine and tomatoes and cook for about 4 minutes, stirring constantly. Add the olives, basil, yellow pepper, capers and salt to taste. Mix it all together, cover and simmer for approximately 20 minutes. Meanwhile, cook the vermicelli until *al dente*. Drain and transfer to a warm bowl, pour over the sauce and toss together. Serve with grated Caciocavallo or Pecorino to taste.

Serves 4

PIZZA · PIZZA

FOCACCIA ALLA SICILIANA · STUFFED SICILIAN BREAD

This is a delicious snack to serve at a buffet or in small wedges with pre-dinner drinks. Fillings vary, but this one is my own favourite.

> 250 g/8 oz strong white flour
> 1 dessertspoon dried yeast, diluted in 3 tablespoons warm water with a pinch of granulated sugar
> 1 egg yolk
> 6 tablespoons olive oil
> 1 large onion, thinly sliced
> 3 tablespoons black olives, stoned and chopped
> 3 ripe fresh tomatoes, peeled and coarsely chopped
> salt and pepper
> 6 fresh basil leaves

Blend the flour and diluted yeast together, add the egg yolk and knead for ten minutes or until you have a smooth, elastic dough – add more water if required. Leave in a warm bowl in a draught-free place to rise for 1 hour, then knock back and knead briefly again with about one third of the oil. Oil a shallow baking tin about 15 cm × 22.5 cm (6 inches × 9 inches). Roll out the dough to the right width but double the length of the tin. Set aside to prove while you prepare the filling. Fry the onion in about half the remaining oil until soft, then spread it on the dough in the tin. Cover with the chopped olives and tomatoes, season with salt and pepper and tear up the basil leaves and arrange them on top. Cover with the remaining dough and seal the edges very carefully closed. Brush the top with the remaining oil and prick the surface in several places with the prongs of a fork. Leave to rest for about 10 minutes then bake in a preheated moderate oven (180°C, 350°F, Gas Mark 4) for about 25–35 minutes or until golden and crisp. Serve hot or cold.

Serves 4

IL RISO · RICE

RISO E MELANZANE ALLA PALERMITANA · LAYERED RICE AND AUBERGINE BAKE

All the oriental influences are found in this combination of rice and aubergines, a delicious speciality from the city of Palermo.

> 3 large aubergines, sliced
> 2 medium-sized onions, peeled
> 50 g/2 oz butter
> 8 tablespoons olive oil
> fistful of fresh parsley, washed and chopped
> 6 basil leaves, washed and chopped
> 300 g/10 oz fresh ripe tomatoes, peeled, deseeded and chopped
> salt and pepper
> 300 g/10 oz risotto rice
> 600 ml/1 pint broth, boiling hot
> 3 level tablespoons plain white flour
> oil for deep frying
> 6 heaped tablespoons grated Caciocavallo cheese

Put the aubergine slices in a colander and scatter with salt. Put a weight on top and stand the colander in the sink for 1–2 hours so all the bitter juices flow out. Boil the 2 whole onions in water for about 10 minutes then drain and set aside. Heat the butter and 3 tablespoons of the oil in a casserole; when the butter sizzles add one of the onions, finely sliced, and the herbs and tomatoes. Season and cover, simmer gently until required.

In a second ovenproof dish, fry the other onion, chopped, in the remaining olive oil until translucent, then add the rice and turn it so it fries all over. Pour over the boiling hot broth and bring back to the boil, then cover and place in a preheated moderate oven (180°C, 350°F, Gas Mark 4) for 15 minutes. Add more liquid if necessary.

Meanwhile, drain and dry the aubergines, toss them in the flour and deep fry until crisp. Drain and set to one side. Remove the rice from the oven and stir in about one-third of the cheese. With a little of the oil from the aubergines, grease an ovenproof dish and begin to arrange the aubergines, rice and tomato mixture in layers, beginning and ending with aubergines. Cover with the remaining grated Caciocavallo. Bake in a preheated hot oven (200°C, 400°F, Gas Mark 6) for 10 minutes. Serve at once.

Serves 4

I LEGUMI · VEGETABLES

FICATO D'ISETTI CANNOLA · FRIED PUMPKIN WITH MINT

The main market square of the town of Palermo has seven fountains (*setti cannola*) and the name of this dish literally translates as 'liver of the seven fountains', meaning the liver dish of a poor man who could not afford the real thing and bought cheap old pumpkin at the market of the seven fountains then cooked it as if it were liver.

500 g/1 lb yellow pumpkin
oil for deep frying

4 tablespoons wine vinegar
salt
1 teaspoon sugar
7 fresh mint leaves
1 clove garlic, chopped

Peel the pumpkin, remove the seeds and slice into strips no thicker than 1 cm/½ inch. Fry in hot oil until crisp on the outside and soft when pierced with a fork. Pour away most of the oil and pour the vinegar over the pumpkin. Season with salt and sprinkle with the sugar. Add the mint leaves and garlic, turn the slices over to absorb these flavours and cook for 10 minutes before serving.

Serves 4

FRITEDDA · ARTICHOKE AND BROAD BEAN CASSEROLE

6 globe artichokes, trimmed
1 lemon, sliced
1 small onion, chopped
4 tablespoons olive oil
1 kg/2 lb fresh broad beans (with pods)
500 g/1 lb fresh peas (with pods)
salt and pepper
nutmeg
10 fresh mint leaves, chopped
large pinch of sugar
2 teaspoons strong wine vinegar

Cut the artichokes into segments, cover with cold water and add the lemon slices. Fry the onion in the oil until translucent, then drain the artichokes and add to the pan. Cook for a few minutes, then shell the broad beans and peas and add them too. Season with salt, pepper and nutmeg, stir and cover with a lid. Leave to simmer gently, adding a little water if necessary. When the vegetables are tender, add the mint, sugar and vinegar. Cook for a further 5 minutes, then turn out on to a platter and cool completely before serving.

Serves 6

PEPERONI IMBOTTITI · STUFFED PEPPERS

In every Sicilian household this traditional family dish will be prepared in a different way with different fillings. It is just as Sicilian as all the swordfish and pasta dishes, a delicious and satisfying speciality.

> 4 very large green peppers or 8 small ones
> 300 g/10 oz stale bread, crusts removed
> 625 g/1¼ lb canned tomatoes, deseeded and chopped
> 1 tablespoon capers (preferably salted), washed and chopped
> 50 g/2 oz green olives, stoned and sliced
> salt and pepper
> fistful of fresh parsley, chopped
> 2 salted or 4 canned anchovies, filleted and chopped
> 75 g/3 oz Pecorino cheese, grated
> 1 wine glass olive oil

Wash and dry the peppers, then remove the stems and carefully scoop out the inside seeds and membranes. Soften the bread in a little water, then mix in 3 chopped tomatoes and the capers, olives, seasoning, parsley, anchovies, cheese and about 3 table-spoons of the oil. Mix together very thoroughly then spoon the mixture inside the peppers. Pour the remaining oil into an oven-proof dish and scatter the remaining tomatoes over it. Set the peppers upright in the dish and bake for 1 hour in a cool oven

(150°C, 300°F, Gas Mark 2), basting often with the tomato and oil sauce which will form around them. Serve immediately.

Serves 4

INSALATA DI ARANCE · ORANGE SALAD

This fresh, cleansing and pure orange salad flavoured with a hint of leek is just what's needed in the midst of all the rather oily, rich and very lusty Sicilian dishes.

> **6 oranges, preferably blood oranges**
> **1 medium-sized leek**
> **fistful of fresh parsley, finely chopped**
> **5 tablespoons virgin olive oil (or to taste)**
> **salt and pepper**

Peel the oranges right down to the flesh with a small sharp knife, then using a large sharp knife slice them into discs, quite thickly but evenly. Trim and wash the leek, then slice it neatly into discs too. Mix the oranges and leek together and scatter the parsley over. Pour over the olive oil, season with salt and pepper, toss together once and leave to marinate for about 10 minutes before serving. This makes a good accompaniment to rich and oily dishes.

Serves 6

I PESCI · FISH

SARDINE CON IL FINOCCHIO · SARDINES WITH FENNEL

Fennel seeds are used to give this dish its very special flavour.

> **16 small fresh sardines, gutted**
> **olive oil**
> **juice of 1 lemon**
> **salt and pepper**
> **approximately 1 teaspoon fennel seeds, crushed in a**
> **pestle and mortar or processed**
> **fistful of fresh parsley, chopped**
> **50 g/2 oz lard**
> **1 whole lemon, cut into wedges**

Clean the sardines carefully, then rub them lightly with olive oil. Put them in a dish, pour the lemon juice over and season with salt and pepper. Mix the crushed fennel seeds and chopped parsley with the lard. Spread this mixture over each fish and wrap them in twos in baking parchment. Place the packages containing the fish on to a rack in a cool oven (150°C, 300°F, Gas Mark 2) until the paper puffs up and the kitchen is filled with a wonderful perfume of fennel (about 15 minutes). Serve at once, still wrapped in paper, so each person has 2 parcels, with wedges of lemon.

Serves 4

BRACIOLE DI PESCE SPADA · STUFFED SWORDFISH ROLLS

No Sicilian menu would be complete without swordfish. This recipe is originally a speciality of Messina, although variations on it are served around Palermo and Catanzaro. Swordfish is caught only between April and September, when it follows the same itinerary it has followed for centuries, gathering in large shoals in the Mediterranean from the Sargasso sea and crossing through the Strait of Messina. Besides its delicious flavour and texture and the enormous variety of dishes that can be cooked with it, swordfish is an integral part of Sicilian culture, and the hunting of it is essential to the macho lifestyle of the island.

1 onion, thinly sliced
2 tablespoons olive oil
2 cloves garlic, chopped
250 g/8 oz swordfish in very thin steaks, plus 150 g/5 oz swordfish trimmings
fistful of fresh basil, chopped
fistful of fresh parsley, chopped
125 g/4 oz toasted breadcrumbs
1 tablespoon capers, washed and chopped
125 g/4 oz Provolone Piccante or other mature strong cheese, cubed
2 eggs
salt
red chilli powder

FOR THE SAUCE
250 ml/8 fl oz best olive oil
½ wine glass hot water
juice of 2 lemons
1 level tablespoon chopped fresh parsley
1 heaped teaspoon dried oregano
1 clove garlic, crushed

Fry the onion in the olive oil until just blond, add the garlic and the fish trimmings, stir and simmer for a couple of minutes, then add the basil, parsley, breadcrumbs and capers. Cook for a further 2 minutes, then mince the mixture finely. Add the cheese and the eggs and season to taste with salt and chilli.

Flatten the swordfish steaks out as thinly as possible with a meat hammer or the side of a very heavy knife, then spread the stuffing evenly over each steak. Roll up and secure each one with 2 toothpicks. Grill the *braciole* for about 7 minutes, dousing them with the sauce.

To make the sauce, pour the olive oil into a bowl and whisk it constantly as you pour in the hot water and lemon juice. Keep whisking and add the parsley and oregano, then the crushed garlic clove. The sauce must end up velvety smooth and evenly textured. Heat until just warm over a bain-marie and then use to douse the fish under the grill. This sauce can also be used to dress roasted meat, other kinds of fish, and all sorts of grilled food.

Serves 4

CAPONATA DI SCAMPI E MOLLUSCHI · SICILIAN SEAFOOD SALAD

Like swordfish dishes, *caponata* is a traditional part of Sicilian cuisine. This is an immensely laborious and complex dish, and consequently one you're not likely to come across very often. It was originally from Spain, and has evolved from being a poor dish – just a combination of fish and vegetables – into this rich and very elaborate masterpiece.

> **4 aubergines**
> **salt**
> **1 carrot, scraped and cut into 4**
> **1 onion, peeled and cut into 4**
> **1 celery stick, washed and cut in half**
> **1 tablespoon white wine vinegar**
> **5 sprigs fresh parsley, washed and trimmed**

3 sprigs fresh thyme, washed and trimmed
2 bay leaves
1 live lobster
oil for deep frying
4 celery hearts
plain white flour
300 g/10 oz button onions
4 tablespoons olive oil
2 tablespoons granulated sugar
2 tablespoons red wine vinegar
500 g/1 lb fresh ripe tomatoes, peeled, deseeded and
coarsely chopped
fistful of fresh parsley, finely chopped
2 cloves garlic, finely chopped
1 tablespoon capers, washed and chopped
300 g/10 oz squid or octopus (small and tender)
250 g/8 oz black or green olives, stoned
salt and pepper
300 g/10 oz raw prawns
4 eggs, hard boiled, shelled and sliced

FOR THE SAUCE
3 tablespoons cooking oil
125 g/4 oz blanched almonds
50 g/2 oz stale toast, reduced to fine crumbs
3 salted or canned anchovies, filleted and washed
juice of 1 orange
25 g/1 oz granulated sugar
25 g/1 oz powdered chocolate
½ wine glass red wine vinegar
½ wine glass water

Slice the aubergines into discs, put them in a large colander, sprinkle with salt and put the colander in the sink. Cover with a plate, put a weight on top, and leave them to drain out their bitter juices. Fill a fish kettle or large saucepan with enough water to cover the lobster; add salt and the carrot, onion, celery, white wine vinegar and herbs. Bring to the boil then toss in the live lobster, being sure to immerse it head first. Cover and cook for 15 minutes, then turn off the heat and leave to cool down in the water.

Dry the aubergine slices and deep fry them in oil until crisp and golden, then drain and set aside. Slice the celery hearts downwards to the base but without cutting through the base. Toss them in flour and fry in the oil; they should end up looking like bows when you drain them. Set aside with the fried aubergines.

Bring about 250 ml/8 fl oz salted water to the boil, peel the button onions and boil them in the water for 10 minutes, then drain. Heat the olive oil in a large saucepan then tip in the partially cooked button onions and brown them all over. Dust with the sugar and let them caramelize, then pour the red wine vinegar over and let it partially evaporate. Lower the heat to minimum, cover and cook for a few minutes, then add the chopped tomatoes and stir. Cook for about 30 minutes, adding a little water if the mixture appears to be drying out. Meanwhile, mix the chopped parsley, garlic and capers together and set aside. Slice the squid or octopus lengthways, in the direction of the tentacles, toss them in flour and deep fry until crisp, then drain and set aside. Add the parsley, garlic and caper mixture to the onions and tomatoes. Mix carefully, then add the olives and mix again. Season to taste, then add the fried aubergines and fried celery hearts. Leave this mixture simmering under a lid.

Remove the lobster from the water, split open the tail, remove all the meat and cut into thin strips. Add the fried squid or octopus and the sliced lobster to the tomato and aubergine mixture, stirring it gently and keeping it all gently simmering. When it is all mixed up, tip the whole lot out on to a large platter and leave to cool. Cook the prawns quickly in boiling salted water or in the lobster stock, which must first be brought to the boil. After 5 minutes drain the prawns and set aside. Arrange the cooled aubergine mixture into a dome shape on a new platter and cover completely with the sauce (see below), smoothing it carefully over the whole of it. Decorate with the cooled prawns, the sliced hardboiled eggs and the meat from the rest of the lobster. Serve.

To make the sauce, heat the oil in a small saucepan, add the almonds and brown carefully all over. When they are quite dark, drain them, put them in a mortar or food processor and reduce to a fine powder with the toast crumbs. Add the anchovies and orange juice, then the sugar and chocolate, a little at a time. When all is well amalgamated, place in a small saucepan (preferably not aluminium) and add the vinegar and water. Mix together very thoroughly and place over a low heat. Stirring all the time, cook the sauce for 5 minutes, then strain. Use to cover the *caponata*.

Serves 10–12

PESCI SPADA A GHIOTTA · SWORDFISH CASSEROLE

This is another recipe from Messina, where swordfish has been cooked in this way for many centuries. There are a few interesting variations you may like to try. The addition of fresh peas is very popular, and in many parts of the island they leave out the pine nuts and sultanas and substitute black olives with the triangular part of the fish from the centre of its breast.

Sultanas and currants, all used to a large degree in Sicilian cuisine, come from Greece. The local raisins, on the other hand, are from the island of Pantelleria and are used in baking and pastry making as well as being eaten as dried fruits in their own right.

> 25 g/1 oz sultanas
> 4 slices swordfish
> 2 level tablespoons plain white flour
> oil for frying
> 1 onion, chopped

2 cloves garlic, chopped
25 g/1 oz pine kernels
1 large celery stick, finely chopped
1 tablespoon capers (preferably salted), washed
1 handful green olives in brine, stoned
400 g/13 oz fresh ripe tomatoes, peeled, deseeded and chopped
salt and pepper
2 bay leaves
slices of coarse bread, toasted

Cover the sultanas in cold water and leave to soak. Coat the fish lightly in the flour and fry in sizzling oil until sealed and golden. Drain, then set aside. In the oil in which the fish was cooked, fry the chopped onion with the garlic until golden. Drain and dry the sultanas, add to the pan with the pine kernels, celery, capers and olives. Stir together and cook for a few minutes. Then add the tomatoes and seasoning and simmer under a lid for about 10 minutes. Arrange the fish in an ovenproof dish and cover with the sauce. Add the bay leaves and bake for 15 minutes in a pre-heated hot oven (200°C, 400°F, Gas Mark 6). Serve with the slices of toasted coarse bread.

Serves 4

LE CARNI · MEAT

SCALOPPINE DI MAIALE AL MARSALA · PORK LOIN WITH MARSALA

Marsala, that most typical of all Sicilian wines, is used in a sauce to serve with pork escalopes in this dish to make a lovely combination of flavours.

20 g/¾ oz lard
2 tablespoons olive oil
1 clove garlic, peeled and crushed
500 g/1 lb boned pork loin steaks, sliced and trimmed
salt and pepper
20 g/¾ oz butter
1 level tablespoon plain white flour
1 wine glass dry Marsala

Heat the lard and oil together with the garlic, remove the garlic as soon as it is brown, then lay the meat in the hot fat and brown it all over. Season. Remove the meat when it is cooked through, and keep it warm while you prepare the Marsala sauce. Blend the butter and flour together in a bowl and pour the Marsala into the pan in which the meat was cooked. Bring to the boil then mix in the butter and flour and stir to a smooth consistency. Pour over the pork and serve.

Serves 4

FILETTO DI VITELLO ALLA MESSINESE · MESSINA VEAL

700 g/1 lb 7 oz veal fillet, cut into 4 very thick steaks
75 g/3 oz pork fat, cut into long, thin strips
8 tablespoons olive oil
1 onion, chopped
50 g/2 oz prosciutto crudo (Parma ham), chopped
1 carrot, washed and scraped
1 sprig fresh parsley
1 sprig fresh basil
1 sprig fresh sage
1 sprig fresh celery leaves
salt and pepper
1 large glass dry white wine

2 yellow peppers
2 large ripe tomatoes
2 slices white bread, cut in half

Trim the veal and wrap each steak with one or two strips of pork fat, tying them on with thread. Heat 3 tablespoons of the oil and fry the onion and prosciutto in it until golden, then brown the veal steaks all over in this pan. Remove the steaks and set aside; transfer the onion and prosciutto to an ovenproof casserole. Add the carrot with the parsley, basil, sage and celery tied around it. Lay the meat on top, season and pour over the wine. Cover with a well-fitting lid and bake in a preheated warm oven (160°C, 325°F, Gas Mark 3). Meanwhile scald the peppers and peel off the skin, split them open, remove the seeds and membranes, and cut into long strips. Peel and deseed the tomatoes, and cut them into strips also. After the meat has been in the oven for 1 hour, scatter the peppers and tomatoes over the top. Cover again and cook for a further 30 minutes.

Fry the bread slices in the remaining oil and keep warm. To serve, arrange the meat and the juices in the centre of a dish, place the bread around it and cover with the cooked peppers and tomatoes.

Serves 4

I POLLI · POULTRY AND GAME

POLLO ALLA MESSINESE · MESSINA CHICKEN WITH TUNA FISH

This is the way chicken is traditionally prepared in Messina, simply boiled with herbs then served with a deliciously sharp sauce flavoured with tuna, anchovies and capers.

3 celery sticks
fistful of fresh parsley
fistful of fresh basil
salt
1 boiling fowl or chicken, weighing approximately
3 kg/6 lb, or larger
mayonnaise made with juice of 1 lemon and 1 egg yolk,
if made by hand, or whole egg if made in food
processor
90 g/3½ oz canned tuna
2 salted or 4 canned anchovies, filleted and chopped
1 tablespoon capers (preferably salted), washed and
chopped
1 tablespoon wine vinegar (optional)
parsley and basil leaves to garnish

Put the celery, parsley and basil into a saucepan which contains enough water and is large enough to boil the chicken. Bring to the boil, then add the chicken. Salt the water and let the chicken cook gently for about 1½ hours. Meanwhile make the lemon mayonnaise and flake the tuna. Push the tuna, anchovies and capers through a sieve (or purée in a food processor) then mix into the mayonnaise very thoroughly. Taste it and if it isn't very sharp add the vinegar. Stir, then refrigerate. Remove the cooked chicken from the water and carve off all the best parts, legs, breast, etc. Arrange them on a platter and leave to cool completely, then pour the sauce over the chicken to cover it completely. Garnish with parsley and basil leaves, then serve.

Serves 6–8

POLLO ALLA CACCIATORA CON MELANZANE · CHICKEN CASSEROLE WITH AUBERGINES

4 aubergines, thickly sliced
salt
125 g/4 oz streaky bacon, chopped
3 tablespoons olive oil
2 cloves garlic, chopped
1.5 kg/3 lb chicken, jointed
1 glass dry white wine
300 g/10 oz fresh ripe tomatoes, peeled, deseeded and chopped
salt and pepper
oil for deep frying
fistful of fresh parsley, finely chopped

Arrange the aubergine slices in a large colander and sprinkle generously with salt. Leave in the sink under a plate with a weight on top for 1–2 hours for all the bitter juices to drain out. Fry the chopped bacon with the oil and garlic until browned, then add the chicken portions and brown on all sides. Pour over the wine and let it evaporate quickly, then add the tomatoes and seasoning. Stir and cover, then leave to cook gently for about 30 minutes. Meanwhile, dry the aubergines and deep fry in hot oil until golden. Drain on paper then add to the chicken. Stir together and finish off the cooking (about another 5–10 minutes). Just before serving, scatter the chopped parsley all over the dish.

Serves 6

CONIGLIO A PURTUISA · SICILIAN-PORTUGUESE RABBIT STEW

Purtuisa is the Sicilian dialect word for Portuguese. In this case it refers to a very elaborate rabbit stew which must have found its way here either via Spain and the Spanish barons or via South America along with chocolate and coffee. The addition of aubergines, however, makes it completely Sicilian in style, whatever its origins might have been. With its usual flair, Sicilian cuisine manages to turn something as basic as a rabbit stew into something really special.

> 200 g/7 oz aubergines, cubed
> oil for deep frying
> 200 g/7 oz potatoes, peeled and sliced
> 1 very large green pepper, washed, deseeded and sliced into large pieces
> 4 fresh mint leaves
> 4 fresh basil leaves
> 2 cloves garlic, peeled
> ½ glass olive oil
> 2 wild rabbits jointed/weight approx. 1.4 kg/2 lb 13 oz
> 1 celery heart, thinly sliced
> 150 g/5 oz onions, thinly sliced
> 50 g/2 oz stoned green olives
> 1 level tablespoon capers
> 500 ml/17 fl oz good stock
> 200 g/7 oz canned tomatoes, sieved
> 2 level tablespoons sugar
> 2 small glasses wine vinegar
> salt and pepper

Put the cubed aubergines into a colander, add salt, then place in the sink with a plate on top for about 30 minutes while the bitter juices drain out. Meanwhile heat the oil for deep frying, and when it is very hot fry the potatoes until crisp. Lift them out then fry the pepper. Dry the aubergines and fry them also. Put the potatoes, green pepper and aubergines on kitchen paper to drain. Chop the mint, basil and garlic together and set aside. Heat the olive oil in a large casserole dish and brown the rabbit pieces in it over a high flame. Remove the rabbit and add the celery, onions, olives and capers, to the casserole. Fry gently for about 5 minutes, then return the rabbit to the pot with the aubergines, potatoes and pepper. Bring the stock to the boil, pour it over the rabbit, then stir in the sieved tomatoes, sugar, vinegar and chopped mint, basil and garlic. Season with salt and pepper, cover and leave to simmer gently for 1 hour over a low heat, stirring occasionally, until the rabbit is tender.

Serves 8

BECCAFICU NNA CIPUDDA · PIGEONS BAKED IN ONIONS

This is an example of poor Sicilian cuisine, with the birds buried inside large onions and cooked just in olive oil and the onion juices.

> **8 very large round onions**
> **8 warblers or small pigeons, gutted and oven ready**
> **1 wine glass olive oil**
> **salt and pepper**
> **2 tablespoons wine vinegar**

Cut the tops off the onions and remove the middle sections so they become hollow. Discard the middles but reserve the onion tops. Rub the birds with half the oil, season with salt and pepper and push them inside the onions. Cover with the onion tops and secure with toothpicks. Put the onions in an oiled ovenproof dish, cover with a tight-fitting lid and bake in a preheated warm oven

(160°C, 325°F, Gas Mark 3) for 1½ hours. Remove from the oven, extract the birds from the onions and arrange them around the birds. Sprinkle with the vinegar and the remaining oil before serving.

Serves 4

I DOLCI · DESSERTS, PIES AND PASTRIES

CASSATA ALLA SICILIANA · SICILIAN CASSATA

The most classical of all the Sicilian ice creams is this ancient dessert which arrived here long ago from the Arab lands where it was known as 'quas'at', which literally means large round bowl. Nuns perfected its creation, until in the sixteenth century religious authorities banned its preparation within convent walls because the good sisters were neglecting their duties as a result of the enormous demand for the delicious cassata.

> 250 g/8 oz granulated sugar
> 1 vanilla pod
> 4 tablespoons water
> 800 g/1 lb 10 oz fresh Ricotta cheese
> pinch of cinnamon
> 150 g/5 oz dark cooking chocolate, chopped
> 500 g/1 lb candied fruit
> 1 heaped tablespoon chopped pistachios
> 2 tablespoons maraschino liqueur
> 500 g/1 lb sponge cake (preferably Genoese sponge)
> 8 tablespoons apricot jam
> 5 level tablespoons icing sugar
> 200 g/7 oz fondant sugar
> 3 tablespoons orange flower water

Put the granulated sugar, vanilla pod and water in a small saucepan over a low heat to melt. When the sugar is completely liquid, remove the vanilla pod. Push the Ricotta twice through a sieve into a bowl and whisk energetically until smooth and creamy. When it resembles whipped cream add the melted sugar a little at a time, whisking constantly, then stir in the cinnamon, chocolate and 200 g/7 oz of the candied fruit, chopped, saving the best pieces for decoration. Finally mix in the pistachios and maraschino liqueur.

Slice the cake finely and use to line a 25 cm/10 inch cake tin, sticking it on with half the apricot jam. Pour the Ricotta mixture into the lined cake tin. Smooth down lightly and cover with the rest of the sliced sponge. Place in the fridge for about 6 hours.

Cut out a 25 cm/10 inch circle of stiff cardboard and one of greaseproof paper. Put the rest of the apricot jam in a saucepan with the icing sugar and let it boil gently until stringy – test by pulling out a little on the point of a knife, dipping in cold water, then holding between finger and thumb. Open up your finger and thumb to see if it is tacky. Take the cassata out of the fridge, place the card and paper on the top, then invert it and turn it out on to a platter. Spread the apricot jam and icing sugar mixture all over it with a spatula. Melt the fondant sugar in a small pan with the orange flower water over a very low heat, stirring constantly. When it is smooth, pour into the centre of the cassata and spread all over very carefully and thoroughly. Leave to set, transfer to a serving platter and decorate with the remaining candied fruit.

Serves 8

CASSATELLE DI PASQUA · SICILIAN TURNOVERS

These extremely rich little pastries are served at Easter and have a delicious chocolaty, spicy filling mixed with Ricotta.

> 300 g/10 oz fine plain white flour
> pinch of salt
> 1 level tablespoon granulated sugar
> 30 g/1¼ oz butter, cubed
> 1 egg
> grated zest of 1 orange
> grated zest of ½ lemon
> 125 g/4 oz dark cooking chocolate, chopped
> 300 g/10 oz Ricotta cheese, sieved
> 150 g/5 oz caster sugar
> oil for deep frying
> 5 tablespoons icing sugar
> 2 pinches of cinnamon

Sieve the flour on to the table. Add the salt and sugar and mix together. Add the butter, egg, grated orange and lemon zest and a drop of water. Knead together until smooth and elastic, wrap in a tea towel and leave to one side for about 20 minutes to rest.

Meanwhile, mix the chopped chocolate with the Ricotta and the caster sugar until it has a smooth, homogenous texture. Roll out the dough to a 2 mm/⅛ inch thickness, using only a little of it at a time. Cut into circles about 10 cm/4 inches across and place a tablespoonful of the mixture on each one. Fold the pastry over so as to make little half-moon shapes. Pinch shut very carefully so that none of the filling can escape. Heat the oil in a deep fryer and fry the *cassatelle* about 4 at a time until crisp and golden. Drain on kitchen paper, sift icing sugar and cinnamon over them and serve either tepid or cold.

Makes 30

SPUMETTE DI NOCCIOLE · HAZELNUT MERINGUES

These light and delicious little hazelnut meringues are prepared all over Sicily in various forms. In some places they are known as *sospiri di monaca* – nun's sighs. The myth of the nuns being trapped in convents fantasizing about what they've missed out on because of their vow of chastity is very popular all over Italy. There is a kind of plum called nun's buttocks, a variety of bread rolls called nun's breasts, and various other slightly warped popular sayings relating to the good sisters and whatever is believed they do and feel within the convent walls.

200 g/7 oz blanched hazelnuts
4 egg whites
300 g/10 oz icing sugar
grated zest of 1 lemon
butter for greasing

Chop or process the hazelnuts as finely as possible. Beat the egg whites until very stiff and dry, gradually adding the sifted icing sugar. Carefully fold in the hazelnuts and lemon zest. Grease a baking tray and spoon out the meringue into neat piles about 5 cm/2 inches apart. Put in a very cool oven (100°C, 200°F, Gas Mark ¼) for about 2 hours. They must be dry but still white.

Makes about 30–40

BUDINO DI RISO E CASTAGNE · RICE AND CHESTNUT PUDDING

This creamy rice pudding is very unlikely for Sicily, yet delicious and wonderful. The south is always full of surprises.

75 g/3 oz dried chestnuts
1 litre/1¾ pints milk

    salt
    50 g/2 oz sultanas
    50 g/2 oz sugar
    150 g/5 oz pudding rice
    75 g/3 oz butter
    2 tablespoons fresh white breadcrumbs
    8 candied violets
    4 marrons glacés

Cover the dried chestnuts with cold water and leave to soak for a day. Drain, remove any bits of skin left attached, and put them in a saucepan with the milk and a pinch of salt. Bring to the boil and simmer slowly until soft. Cover the sultanas with cold water and leave to soak for 15 minutes. Drain and add to the chestnuts with the sugar and rice. Cook slowly for about 20 minutes, until the rice is soft. If it is too dry mix in a little hot milk. Stir in three-quarters of the butter then remove from the heat.

    Grease a pudding mould with the rest of the butter and scatter with the breadcrumbs to coat thoroughly. Pour in the pudding mixture, cool, and refrigerate for about 3 hours. Before serving, turn out on to a platter and decorate with candied violets and crumbled marrons glacés.

Serves 6

CUCCIADATU · CHOCOLATE AND NUT PASTRIES

These very rich, filling pastries are stuffed to bursting with various kinds of dried fruit, nuts and other goodies. They vary in size throughout the island, either huge and round with a diameter of 60–80 cm (2 feet–2 feet 8 inches), or small and delicate.

    500 g/1 lb strong plain flour
    pinch of salt

200 g/7 oz sugar
300 g/10 oz fresh unsalted butter, plus extra for greasing
4 eggs
325 g/11 oz dried soft figs, chopped
150 g/5 oz shelled walnuts, chopped
150 g/5 oz blanched almonds, chopped
125 g/4 oz sultanas
50 g/2 oz pistachios
250 g/8 oz orange marmalade
50 g/2 oz bitter chocolate, chopped
1 level teaspoon cinnamon
3 cloves, chopped
rind of ½ orange, finely sliced

Sift the flour on to the table with the salt and sugar, then knead in the butter and 3 of the eggs. Don't mix it too much, just enough to bind the ingredients. Wrap it up in lightly oiled tinfoil and put in the refrigerator until required. Meanwhile, mix all the other ingredients together, including the remaining egg.

Remove the dough from the fridge and roll it out to about 3 mm/⅙ inch thick. Cut into 12 rounds about 20–30 cm/8–12 inches across and lay them on buttered baking trays. Spoon some of the filling mixture into the centre of each one, pulling the edges up and over slightly so you half cover the filling with pastry. Bake in a preheated moderate oven (180°C, 350°F, Gas Mark 4) for 30 minutes. Serve warm or cold.

Makes 12

THE WINES OF SICILY

There are over forty bottled and labelled wines produced on this magical island, all of them well worth sampling, not to mention the countless unlabelled carafe wines you are likely to be served locally. The Greeks, Normans and even the invading Saracens told stories about these wines, and their quality and flavour was famous for centuries all over the known world.

There is the famous Marsala; the pure wine called Etna, which owes its special, cleansing flavour to the volcano's lava in the soil; the aristocratic Fara wines from Messina, ruby-red and shining clear, perfect with the locally shot game; and then the enormous wealth of sweet dessert wines for which the island is so well known. Other distinguished wines include the incredibly heady Mammertino, which has the scent of a bunch of freshly picked violets and the colour of ancient gold; the Malvasias from Lipari, Salina and Stomboli, which grand ladies in the great Sicilian novels sip at the end of their meals, whilst nibbling a fine almond biscuit; and then the Zucco d'Oro, the Moscato from Pantelleria and from Siracusa, and the Passito from Misilmeri. There are hot, scorching wines that are filled with the island's passion, born of its almost permanently clear blue skies and the burning sun.

Here are a few of the labels the island produces:

Albanello di Siracusa A dessert wine produced in the Siracusa province with Albanello secco and Albanello dolce grapes. It is reminiscent of Marsala, with a dry, generous flavour.

Alcano Bianco This comes from the Alcano area – one of the main wine-producing zones of Sicily. It is largely used for making vermouth or as a cutting wine (*vino da Taglio*) to add flavour and depth to other wines. A limited quantity is kept for producing a really excellent table wine with a strange, mother-of-pearl colour, a delicate, slightly aromatic herby bouquet and a full, solid flavour that marries perfectly with all strong-tasting Sicilian fish dishes.

Ambrato di Comiso An amber-coloured dessert wine currently enjoying a big comeback after being almost completely ignored for several decades.

Capo Bianco This wine is from an area around Milazzo with vines that have only recently been introduced to the area. There is a white and a rosé version and both are delicious table wines, particularly the rosé.

Cerasulo di Vittoria A bright-red, fizzing, foaming wine that perfectly encapsulates the very spirit of Sicily with its hot, slightly tannic flavour and very decisive, rich bouquet. Excellent with game when aged about three years.

Eloro bianco and Eloro rosso Two very special table wines from the Noto area, both dry and really delicious.

Etna wine comes in a white, red or rosé version – all three are rich, pure wines, bursting with fragrance and passion.

Mammertino Another dessert wine, praised by Pliny and Martial in a time when sweet wines were definitely preferred and drunk much more freely than dry northern wines – a sweet wine meant it had been sun-warmed by the shores of the Mediterranean. Mammertino is a special combination of grapes, including a small quantity of the Spanish Pedro Ximenes. There is also a fabulous dry white version produced in the area which is drunk with fish and throughout any typical Sicilian meal.

Marsala This is one of the island's most famous wines, if not one of the most famous in the world. At the height of Sicily's Belle Epoque in the late nineteenth century, two English families, the Whitakers and the Inghams, made vast fortunes by exporting this wine to England. It comes in several versions, ranging from as dry as the driest sherry to as sticky and sweet as a cordial. Top of the range is Marsala superiore; available in dry *amabile* or sticky-sweet versions, it is a very high quality wine with a price to match.

Marsala speciale is Marsala to which other ingredients such as cream, sultanas and coffee beans have been added. Marsala all'uovo is Marsala with egg, which makes it especially good for invalids. Marsala fine is much less coarse than basic Marsala and is available in varying degrees of sweetness.

Marsala vergine is the driest variety of all and is normally drunk at the start of a meal as an aperitif. Do not serve this wine with chocolate-flavoured desserts; the two flavours clash horribly!

Raro A famous red from the Messina area. It has been enjoyed in its present form at least since the beginning of the nineteenth century. It is ruby coloured, rich and full when young, and improves as it ages, being at its best when about five years old.

Other Sicilian wines include: Malvasia delle Lipari, Moscato di Noto, Moscato di Pantelleria, Moscato di Siracusa, Ombra, Regaleali, Taormina, Torreforti, Val di Lupo, Vini della Piana di Catania, Vini della Piana di Mascali, Aurora, Fontanamurata Bianco, Fontanamurata Rosso, Grecanico, Moscato Zucco, Pachino, Partinico, Val d'Anapo.

EATING OUT IN SOUTHERN ITALY

At the time of writing, a culinary revolution is sweeping Italy, and is most evident in the new restaurants that are cropping up all over the south. The idea behind the change is that the flavour and texture of Italian food should remain unaltered, but that if regional cuisine is to survive at all, the sheer weight and indigestibility of some of the dishes need to be moderated. Although much of southern Italian cuisine is healthy, full of vegetables, seafood, fish and fruit, there are some extremely heavy dishes. I give you the example of a flat loaf of unleavened bread dough, about 7.5–10 cm/3–4 inches thick, lined with raw strips of pork belly, and baked until the fat runs into the dough and becomes one big lump of very greasy, heavy-duty goo. If you eat a couple of slices of *that* local speciality, I guarantee that you'll still be digesting it in fifteen days' time! Someone who spends all day ploughing and farming by hand, does not own or use a car and has no central heating, can afford to eat some of the rib-sticking combinations which used to be a part of day-to-day meals. However, times are changing, and even in the deepest south there is a lot less manual labour being carried out – albeit certainly more than in the north.

So the restaurateurs of the south have begun to adapt and 'lighten' their traditional dishes. The change is very much less obvious in Basilicata, where a kind of suspension in time can be felt, but where you can eat very well provided you like chilli peppers! On the whole, I am delighted to see that far from abandoning their traditions, the locals are determined *not* to internationalize their restaurants, and are sticking to their culinary roots, of which they are so rightfully proud.

CAMPANIA

There are a few basics at the heart of Campanian cooking: they invented and therefore make the very best pizza in the world; they were the first to commercialize pasta on any scale, and claim to have invented this as well – whatever the truth is, the pasta is excellent all over the region; they were the first to cook and eat tomatoes so they use this ingredient to absolute perfection; they are obsessed with coffee making and drinking, and many people will tell you that coffee in Naples tastes better than anywhere else; the excellent soil provided by the proximity of Vesuvius enables huge and delicious fruit and vegetables to be cultivated; wonderful Mozzarella is made here; they also make an enormous variety of cakes and pastries, which almost rival those of Sicily. Armed with all this knowledge, you can't go wrong when you eat out in this joyful, sunny, smiling region. Campanian cooking is, generally speaking, more sophisticated than elsewhere in the south, maybe because of the influence of the royal court at Naples and the French chefs who were brought in by Marie Antoinette's sister, Carolina, during her marriage to Ferdinand I of Bourbon – although the locals will tell you that their dishes are the food of poor people which have developed over the centuries into international favourites.

A favourite restaurant of mine is the Ristorante Da Giovanni in Via Domenico Morelli in Naples, where I can always be confident of sampling the local cuisine at its best. To drink coffee in a historical monument is also possible in Naples if you go to the café Gambrinus in Via Chiaia 1/2, where you can absorb the intellectual atmosphere knowing that D'Annunzio once drank coffee there too.

APULIA

On the whole, the restaurants situated near the sea in Apulia serve excellent fish and seafood, and the local mussels and oysters are purified overnight in water treated with ultraviolet light to make it completely pure. If you venture inland, a great deal of lamb and an awful lot of offal will appear on the menu! Midway through your meal, i.e. after the antipasti and pasta but before the main course, you will be served a large dish of raw vegetables such as cucumber, celery, fennel, radishes, etc., which should be chewed slowly to aid digestion and prepare you for the rest of the meal.

A *rosticceria* is often a restaurant attached to the local butcher's shop, which means that the menu usually consists of the meat left at the end of the day's sales, cooked very simply on long skewers in front of an open fire. Once again, do be prepared to be served a great deal of offal in places such as these. Alternatives include deliciously fresh, succulent chunks of lamb roasted on a wood fire. These restaurants tend to be the equivalent of a *trattoria* or *osteria*, in local terms. In coastal towns such as Bari and Taranto you can buy very fresh seafood to eat as you walk along the streets – it is sold raw by street vendors near the port. I suggest you decide for yourself, depending upon the cleanliness and condition of the kiosk, whether you trust the seafood. All over the region you will be served delectable olive oil, excellent fruit and vegetables and very good wine. Not to be forgotten is the attractive, locally produced pasta, both handmade and factory made, which along with savoury pies and cakes has been an important part of the local cuisine for many decades.

BASILICATA

The food served in restaurants around Basilicata tends to remain somewhat old-fashioned, and is generally very fiery thanks to the ever-present chilli peppers. Near the beautiful resort of Maratea you can sample delicious fish and seafood, whereas inland you are likely to be offered a collection of dishes made with very few ingredients but put together with imagination and flair so that they are pretty to look at and delicious to eat. A condiment sits proudly on the table next to the salt and pepper cruet; it is called *olio santo*, holy oil, and is pure olive oil into which a good few strong chillis have been crushed to make it very hot and peppery and of a dark red colour. I can recommend two restaurants in this very small and remote region: Taverna Rovita, right in the historical centre of Maratea in Via Rovita, offers the very best local fare served with pride. A small but carefully put-together menu of delicious local specialities can also be sampled at the Ristorante Moro in Vicolo Quarto Cappellutti 2 in Matera. Matera is well worth a visit if you are in Basilicata, because of the astonishing ancient city made of caves and grottoes dug out of a hill. The bread of Matera is famous all over Italy for its delicious flavour and excellent texture. Interestingly, horseradish crops up in many restaurants – they call it poor man's truffle – and is used in pasta sauces or savoury pies.

CALABRIA

I think that in Calabria, more than in any of the five regions covered in this book, the current food revolution is obvious when you eat out. If you want to experience the changes for yourself, go to Ristorante Alia A Jetticelle, at Via Jetticelle 69, run with fierce passion and great knowledge by ex-doctor Pinuccio Alia, his brother and his mother in their old family home just outside Castrovillari. Here you will eat fourteenth- and sixteenth-century Calabrian dishes updated and reinterpreted in a modern style – delicious food and certainly much easier to digest than some of the local dishes. This is the most famous restaurant in the region, but fortunately other local restaurateurs and cooks are following

Pinuccio Alia's lead and there are many fairly upmarket places where you can enjoy similar dishes. Try cured pork fillet dressed with a light honey and chilli sauce, a raw artichoke salad dressed with juniper vinegar, and many more delicious flavours that taste new but are actually as old as the region itself. In many local restaurants you will see carpaccio of swordfish – raw slivers of swordfish dressed with a light vinaigrette; it is too good to miss! If you go to more old-fashioned, traditional restaurants, such as Conti in Reggio Calabria itself, you will be overpowered by the amount of chilli used by local cooks. It seems to get in everywhere and can become monotonous after a while; it also serves to cover up less-than-fresh flavours.

You are more than likely to come across delicious wild boar prosciutto (*prosciutto di cinghiale*), a wide variety of stuffed peppers, courgettes and aubergines, and a huge and very tasty selection of cured meats and sausages. Near the port of Villa San Giovanniu, before boarding the ferry to cross to Sicily, you'll find a row of excellent restaurants serving very good seafood, swordfish and simple pasta dishes. Particularly good is the Boccaccio Via Pescatori, just along the seafront from the ferry port. The family that runs this rather rough-and-ready outfit catches all its own fish and their mother cooks it for you herself. You can be sure of enjoying very fresh, simply cooked delights here.

SICILY

The quality and flavour of the vegetables and fruit grown in the rich, volcanic soil near Etna means it is very hard to eat badly in this beautiful and culinary-rich island. Every course is bound to be good; the Sicilians are excellent cooks and know how to make everything well, from soups, pasta and rice, to fish and meat dishes and the absolutely magical array of pastries and ice-creams. There is no real tradition of meat cooking here, unlike Apulia, Basilicata or inland Calabria, where at least some mutton or pork is eaten. The very healthy local diet relies on the excellent variety of fish and seafood, from superb fresh tuna and swordfish to the tiny little whitebait available in the spring. Don't go to Sicily expecting good beef or chicken, you won't find it here. Don't ask for polenta, or delicate tagliatelle in a cream and mushroom sauce – they won't know what you are talking about! However, if you order any of the wonderful pasta, rice and fish specialities with plenty of local vegetables, you'll know what makes Sicilians love their island so deeply.

Four restaurants in Sicily spring to mind as being loyal and true to their delightful cuisine: in Siracusa, Ristorante Ionico in Rivera Dionisio il Grande 194; in Agrigento, Trattoria del Vigneto in Via Cavaleri Magazzeni 11; in Trapani, Ristorante P. & G. Via Spalti 1; in Palermo, Ristorante La Botte, in Contrada Lenzitti 416. But the most spectacular place to eat in Sicily has to be the amazing converted convent at Piazza San Domenico in Taormina. In what is now called the San Domenico Palace, which is a historical monument of immense value, 500 years of prayer and meditation have left a lingering atmosphere of such peace and tranquillity that it is hard to leave once you've got there! Many famous people, from Pirandello to Thomas Mann, John Steinbeck to Marlene Dietrich, have been here and savoured the wonderful food, beautiful view and delightful surroundings.

SPECIALIST ITALIAN SHOPS IN THE UK

All the big supermarket chains offer such a huge range of Italian ingredients nowadays that you almost need look no further. Even in the depths of Norfolk where I live I can find nearly everything I need in my local supermarket. However, for more unusual ingredients, such as real Italian sausages, I go to two shops in London where I know I'll always find what I need: Terroni, at 138 Clerkenwell Road, EC1, next door to St Peter's Church and opposite Hatton Garden, and Ferraro, at 90 Leather Lane, EC1, just across the road. In other areas of London there are branches of Camisa at 1a Berwick Street and 61 Old Compton Street in Soho, and also at 53 Charlotte Street, W1. Lina's stores is also in Soho at 18 Brewer Street. Finally there is Luigi's at 60 New Kings Road, SW10, 349 Fulham Road, SW10, and 23 Barrett Street, W1.

Outside London: A de Paola, 196 Cheltenham Road, Bristol; Fazzi Brothers, 232 Clyde Street, Glasgow; Jordons, Upper High Street, Thame; La Trufie, 25 The Street, Ashtead, Surrey; Dropout, 157 Sheffield Road, Barnsley; Bernis, 57 Wellfield Road, Cardiff.

For Calabrian specialities by mail order write to: Pizzimenti snc., Via Giulia 13, Reggio Calabria, telephone 0965 92918. They offer a wide selection of excellent olive oil, wine, honey, preserved vegetables in jars, royal jelly, cured meats, almond cakes and biscuits, dried tomatoes, peppers, figs, olives, cheeses, and homemade jams and marmalades made with the delicious local oranges, all delivered to you by post. They will send you an order form (in Italian) by return.

GLOSSARY

TOMATOES

Canned plum tomatoes are available all over the UK. They are very cheap and versatile. Canned tomatoes can be bought whole or chopped and are usually completely additive-free.

Passata is simply plum tomatoes that have been sieved and puréed. It is available in cartons or bottles, and is a very useful store cupboard standby as it saves a lot of time and effort.

Tomato paste is a blend of concentrated sieved tomatoes reduced to a thick, sweet purée. It is used a lot in southern Italy, where very strong and rather sweet flavours are popular.

Fresh tomatoes Unfortunately the luscious tomatoes available all over Italy are not on sale in the UK. Ripe organically grown tomatoes have at least some of the flavour and richness of a real Italian, sunwarmed fruit.

Dried tomatoes are sold in many good delicatessens, covered in olive oil to keep them moist. Serve them as part of an antipasto with a selection of cold meats.

MUSHROOMS

Wild mushrooms have much more flavour than the cultivated varieties. There are many kinds available at good greengrocers during the season, though the huge wild *porcini* you see in Italy are rarely on sale in the UK.

Funghi porcini (Boletus edulis) These wild, very strongly flavoured mushrooms are sold in small packets, dried, in all good delicatessens. *They need to be soaked for 10–15 minutes in warm water before use.*

PINE KERNELS (PINOLI)

These are the small, soft, oval kernels from the nuts that are buried behind the dinosaur scales on a pine cone. In the UK they are sold in small packets in delicatessens and some super-markets. They feature a great deal in southern Italian cookery and add a delicious crunch and a resinous flavour.

SALUMI

The word *salumi* refers to all cured or preserved meats.

Salame is a type of cured sausage. It is dark in colour with whitish spots of fat. In southern Italy it is usually very spicy and tends to be either blended with chilli or coated with it on the outside.

Prosciutto crudo is raw cured ham – often mistaken for Parma ham, which is raw cured ham specifically from the lovely city of Parma. **Prosciutto cotto** is cooked ham, very similar to English gammon.

Guanciale is the very best kind of Italian bacon, though rather hard to find abroad.

Pancetta is second best to guanciale, but is used in the same way and can be bought quite easily in good delicatessens in the UK. If neither of these is available to you, substitute best-quality, preservative-free streaky bacon.

Mortadella is the biggest of all the Italian cured meats – the slices can be as big as a very large dinner plate. It is quite greasy and heavy with large spots of fat. In Sicily it will almost always have pistachios in it and sometimes pine nuts.

CHEESE

Pecorino is the most common cheese in the south – it is made with ewe's milk and is very strong in flavour, much stronger than Parmesan but of similar texture. Although it is fairly widely available in the UK these days in good delicatessens, if you cannot find it you can use Parmesan.

Parmesan – Parmigiano reggiano or Grana padano These are both hard grating cheeses and their maturity varies enormously – the younger the cheese, the more crumbly it will be. Keep Parmesan *unwrapped* in an airy drawer or dry, well-ventilated box, or hang it up in a muslin bag. *Do not* keep it in the fridge. The discarded whey is used to feed the pigs from which Parma ham is made.

Ricotta, made from the discarded whey of other cheeses such as Provolone or Mozzarella, is also popular for use in cooking. It is creamy and soft, quite bland in flavour and so gets used a lot in desserts as well as savoury dishes.

Caciocavallo is reputedly the oldest form of cheese made in Italy. It is a type of Mozzarella which is allowed to dry out and mature in very large pieces. Its name means horse cheese because it used to be carried astride a horse's back, like saddle-bags, as a double cheese. It is a hard cheese which can be grated or diced. The only possible substitute is a very mature farmhouse Cheddar.

Provolone is probably the biggest of all Italian cheeses and is shaped like a long tube. It is made in various forms – either fairly sweet and bland (Provolone Dolce) or matured and peppery (Provolone Piccante).

Mozzarella is a soft, chewy, white cheese which is sold floating in its own whey. Most large supermarkets now stock very good quality Italian Mozzarella. It is a must for cooking, especially on pizza, and is very widely used in various dishes.

HOMEMADE PASTA (for 1 person)

125 g/4 oz plain white flour
1 large egg
pinch of salt

Pile the flour on to a work surface and make a hole in the centre with your fist. Keep about 25 g/1 oz flour to one side for dusting. Break the egg into the hole in the centre of the flour and add the salt. Using your fingers, begin to incorporate the egg into the flour, gradually widening your stirring circle. When all the flour and egg are blended together, knead energetically and firmly for about 10 minutes or until you have a completely elastic dough. You cannot overknead this dough so don't be afraid to knead for longer. Cover and leave to rest for about 5–10 minutes.

When the dough is really elastic, roll it out as thinly as possible, then fold it in half and roll out again. Each time you fold the dough you should be able to roll it thinner, until eventually you will be able to see through it. Roll and fold it over and over again, using a light touch on your rolling pin, until you hear a snap as the rolling pin goes over the fold. This is the air escaping between the fold and it is the signal that the dough is ready to be cut. For tagliatelle, cut into thin ribbon strips, for ravioli or tortellini cut into squares or circles. Use a sharp knife or a pastry cutter. When the pasta is cut and ready to cook, put it on a lightly floured surface such as a tray and cover with a cloth until required. You could also freeze it on a tray. Remember that this kind of pasta takes very little time to cook, only 3–4 minutes for tagliatelle.

If you have a pasta machine, this will give you very clear instructions on how to get the best results. A hand-turned machine is cheaper than an electric one but it takes longer to make the pasta. A food processor is very useful for making the basic dough. Use the blade attachment to blend the egg, flour and salt to a smooth, elastic dough, then continue as described above.

Dried pasta, such as spaghetti or macaroni, is made with durum wheat and water in factory conditions and cannot be made at home. This is what most Italian households use for everyday eating, saving the egg pasta made by hand for special occasions.

BASIC PIZZA OR BREAD DOUGH

250 g/8 oz strong white bread flour
15 g/½ oz dried yeast or 7 g/¼ oz fresh yeast or ½ sachet Easyblend yeast
warm water (quantity depends on the quality of the flour)
1 level teaspoon fine salt
1 tablespoon olive oil, plus oil for greasing

Pile the flour into a mound on the table top. If using fresh or dried yeast, dilute in a cup with about 4 tablespoons warm water and stand in a warm place until frothy. Make a hole in the centre of the flour with your fist, pour in the diluted yeast, or sprinkle on the Easyblend. Add the salt and the oil, then gradually add enough warm water to make a smooth, elastic dough. Knead firmly and energetically for about 10–15 minutes. The dough is ready when it is completely pliable and does not stick to the work surface. Put it into a bowl, cover with a clean napkin and place it in a warm place to rise for about 1½–2 hours or until doubled in volume. Take it out of the bowl and knock it back, then spread it out with your hands on an oiled baking tray, minimum size 30 cm/12 inches. Alternatively, use as directed in the recipe.

Serves 4

INDEX